THE GOSPEL MIRACLES

OTHER BOOKS BY THE AUTHOR:

Calvin's Doctrine of the Word and Sacrament (Oliver and Boyd)
Many Things in Parables (Oliver and Boyd)
Elijah and Elisha (Oliver and Boyd)
Calvin's Doctrine of the Christian Life (Oliver and Boyd)

THE
GOSPEL MIRACLES

Studies in Matthew, Mark, and Luke

RONALD S. WALLACE

OLIVER AND BOYD

EDINBURGH AND LONDON

1960

OLIVER AND BOYD LTD
Tweedale Court
Edinburgh 1
39A Welbeck Street
London, W.1

The Scripture quotations in this book are from the
Revised Standard Version of the Bible, copy-
righted 1946 and 1952 by the Division of Christian
Education, National Council of the Churches of
Christ in the U.S.A., and used by permission.

FIRST PUBLISHED 1960

PRINTED IN GREAT BRITAIN FOR OLIVER AND BOYD LTD
BY HAZELL WATSON AND VINEY LTD, AYLESBURY AND SLOUGH

To
the members of the
Scottish Church Theology Society

ACKNOWLEDGMENTS

THANKS are due to Messrs. Hodder & Stoughton for permission to quote on page 67 from *Religion, Psychology and Healing* by Dr. Leslie Weatherhead, and to the S.C.M. press for permission to quote on page 109 from D. S. Cairns, *The Faith that Rebels*.

FOREWORD

SOME of these studies were preached in their present form as sermons. Others are longer, more elaborate and closely reasoned than sermons should be. They contain the material of two or more sermons put together in a readable unified homiletic form. The book is an attempt to present in an orderly way the main lines along which I was led when I sought to interpret these miracle stories to my congregation.

What is Jesus Christ saying to the Church today through such passages of Holy Scripture?

Our theologians and scholars have rightly a great deal to say to us in answer to this question. They help us to understand the background and meaning of the text, to judge what should be accepted or rejected in the traditional interpretations that have been handed down in the history of the Church, and to see the relevance of the texts in face of the general issues confronting the Church as a whole. They constantly remind us of what should be central in the message we preach, and indicate to us the mind of Christ as it is revealed in the Bible as a whole. They are called and ordained to their office in order that, through them, the Holy Spirit might guide the Church. Often the preacher will find that the scholars give him all the help he needs, and his task is simply to repeat and make relevant in his own way what they have already said about the text in their way.

But sometimes the preacher will find himself impelled to say something different, even contrary to the guidance given to him by the doctors of the Church. Sometimes he will be constrained to adhere to the plain literal meaning of a text of which they warn him to be suspicious. Sometimes he will be led to preach on a passage which has been neglected or perhaps even deliberately rejected by them, but which has nevertheless gripped his own mind with a power and reality that he cannot shake off. In such ways the situation sometimes arises in which, after listening to everything the scholars have to say, the preacher is left quite alone with the responsibility of deciding what actually a particular passage of Holy Scripture says to the people of God in the name of Christ.

He must believe that where he is actually placed, on the line dividing the pew from the pulpit, the risen Christ is seeking to speak His Word through this particular passage to the men and women of the Church in their concrete life-situations. Therefore he must expect guidance beyond that which is given him by the scholars, or the tradition of the Church. In his mind and heart, as well as in the scholar's, the Easter miracle must take place, of Christ opening the understanding and revealing Himself and His Word to his disciples through the Scriptures.

If the interpretation which he has given to a passage has to have any value for the Church as a whole, it must now be submitted to the scholar for his assessment and criticism. One of our professors of Christian Dogmatics recently wrote: "It is one of the principal tasks of the theologian in each generation to bring the preaching of the Church to the bar of the Word of God, and to test its adequacy as a faithful presentation of the message and teaching of the New Testament."

This is as it should be. At the Reformation there was an extremely close and constant relationship between the pulpit, the lecture room, and the discipline and pastoral life of the Church. These aspects of the Church's activity have tended to fall apart, and in the process the scholar has tended to become an academic specialist whose conclusions have tended to seem remote and authoritarian.

A real place must therefore be kept within the life of the Church for the circulation of the current Biblical exposition that is given from the pulpit. The task of Biblical interpretation is one in which the whole Church must join as one body sharing in its unity in the prophetic ministry of its King and Head. Even the layman should be brought in to share, not simply in the priestly and kingly ministry of Christ in the Church, as he does already, but also in His prophetic ministry. Every minister who has had the privilege of leading a Bible study group in his congregation knows that in the fellowship and discussion of the group insights have been given to him into the meaning of certain passages of Scripture that he could not have gained by himself or from the ocmmentators alone.

Let me now acknowledge my debt to the scholars who helped me as I prepared this book—especially to Julius Schniewind for his commentaries on Matthew and Mark, to Alan Richardson for his, "The Miracle Stories of the Gospels", and to Trench for his "Notes on the Miracles".

I must express my deep appreciation of the work done by my sister, and Miss Dorothea Hofer in typing, and by my wife in correcting the manuscript and reading proofs. I would also like again to express my debt to Messrs. Oliver and Boyd, the publishers, for their help and encouragement.

R. S. WALLACE

Lothian Road Church
Edinburgh
May 1960

CONTENTS

THE MIRACULOUS CATCH OF FISH

While the people pressed upon him to hear the word of God, he was standing by the lake of Gennesaret. And he saw two boats by the lake; but the fishermen had gone out of them and were washing their nets. Getting into one of the boats, which was Simon's, he asked him to put out a little from the land. And he sat down and taught the people from the boat. And when he had ceased speaking, he said to Simon, "Put out into the deep and let down your nets for a catch." And Simon answered, "Master, we toiled all night and took nothing! But at your word I will let down the nets." And when they had done this, they enclosed a great shoal of fish; and as their nets were breaking, they beckoned to their partners in the other boat to come and help them. And they came and filled both the boats, so that they began to sink. But when Simon Peter saw it, he fell down at Jesus' knees, saying, "Depart from me, for I am a sinful man, O Lord." For he was astonished, and all that were with him, at the catch of fish which they had taken; and so also were James and John, sons of Zebedee, who were partners with Simon. And Jesus said to Simon, "Do not be afraid; henceforth you will be catching men." And when they had brought their boats to land, they left everything and followed him.

Lk. v. 1–11

Jesus did this miracle not in order to catch fish, but in order to catch Peter and James and John for His own service. Up to this point these three men had been deeply interested in Jesus. John the Baptist had introduced them to Him. They had come to know something of the power of His influence and the meaning of His teaching. But they were not yet fully committed. They had not yet left all to follow Him. Jesus did this miracle with the sole purpose of persuading them to take this final step, and to show them what this would involve.

In this miracle, Jesus spoke to His disciples by means of an action. He sometimes preferred to speak in this way rather than by words. On the night on which He was betrayed, for instance, He took bread and wine, and in a simple action at the Passover Table He spoke with a meaning deeper than words could utter. So here in this incident He takes a boat and a net and fishes and men and does a miracle in order to say to Peter and James and John some things that He could say in this way

more vividly and memorably than by addressing them directly
with speech.

Today He is still fishing for men, and we in our turn have
to go out to catch others for Him. We can learn how to do it
by watching closely how He did it in His day.

A FRIENDLY APPROACH BY THE LAKESIDE

Boats, nets, fish and the sea were the things that Peter and
James and John understood better than almost anything else
in the world. Therefore Jesus came right down to their level,
and translated what He had to say to them in terms of boats,
nets, fish and the sea. If they had been soldiers He would no
doubt have spoken to them in different terms with a different
kind of miracle. If they had been merchants He might have
spoken to them in terms of trading and profiting, and He might
have added a miracle in the realm of finance. If they had been
men of the hills His miracle might have been done with sheep
and lambs and shepherds. But they were men of the lake, so He
spoke in terms of the fishing world. Our Lord "draws each by
the art which is most familiar and natural to him," says
Chrysostom. Archbishop Trench quotes from a sermon on this
subject by John Donne. "The Holy Ghost speaks in such forms
and such phrases as may most work upon them to whom He
speaks. Of David, that was shepherd before, God says, He took
him to feed His people. To those Magi of the East, who were
given to the study of the stars, God gave a star to be their
guide to Christ at Bethlehem. To those who followed Him to
Capernaum for meat, Christ took occasion by that to preach
to them of the spiritual food of their souls. To the Samaritan
woman whom He found at the well, He preached of the water
of life. To these of our text, accustomed to a joy and gladness
when they took great or small store of fish, He presents His
comforts agreeably to their taste, that they should be fishers
still. Christ makes heaven all things to all men, that He might
gain all."

What has this approach to say to us today, as we seek to win
men for the service of Christ? Christ has seen to it that today
we do not need to boost our appeal to men by trying to do
spectacular miracles in His name. Today we have something
more telling and appealing with which to approach men than

any miracle could be. We have the rich fellowship and tradition of the Church, the power of the Holy Spirit poured out at Pentecost, and the Gospel of the crucified, risen and ascended Lord, nothing of which could have been presented to Simon and his companions in these early days by the lakeside.

But, following the example of Our Lord Himself, we can try to take men as we find them, and to speak to them in terms they will understand. If we are to be fishers of men, we have to remember that fishing requires skill, common sense and at least some attempt to understand the mind and habits of the fish. Men will be prepared to listen to what we have to say if they believe that we know and understand something of the world they live and move and work in. A Church that does not interest itself in the conditions and details of the work that makes up the daily life of the population around its doors, is a Church that has ceased to be as human as Jesus Christ was. A minister of the Gospel who cannot speak to his people as one who understands the background of their daily life and work, with its hardships, disappointments and successes, is also not taking seriously the fact that God became man in Jesus Christ. Jesus often began with men on the level of the familiar.

In decending thus to the fishermen's level Jesus was not ashamed even to borrow and to ask a favour from one of them. *"While the people pressed upon him to hear the word of God, he was standing by the lake of Gennesaret. And he saw two boats by the lake; but the fishermen had gone out of them and were washing their nets. Getting into one of the boats, which was Simon's, he asked him to put out a little from the land. And he sat down and taught the people from the boat."* He was obviously not shy of asking Simon to help, for He got into the boat before He even asked if he was willing to help. Moreover He asked this favour of Simon, even before He knew that Simon was fully committed to become His disciple. Whether committed or uncommitted, however, it is quite certain that Simon Peter would remember the sermon Jesus preached from his own boat that day. This was Jesus's intention. He was ready to put Himself temporarily in debt to this man, if this would help him to become eternally in debt to Himself.

We ourselves are sometimes very nervous in this matter. It is right in the name of Christ to try to make people become interested in the Church by asking favours of them? Should

we ever enlist the help of complete outsiders who may have
no sympathy with our work, and thus put the Church in debt
to the uncommitted and unconverted? When we are preaching
and teaching the Gospel, how much should we go outside the
Bible to borrow language, and ways of speaking, and illustra-
tions from the secular world to which we are speaking? No doubt
a line must be drawn somewhere. But before we draw any line
in any case, let us think of how Jesus put Himself in debt to
Simon before He even knew He had His man.

LAUNCHING INTO THE DEPTHS

Once He was in the boat beside them, Jesus soon made Peter
and the others aware that in accepting and entering His
friendship they were allowing themselves to be led beyond
their depths into the mystery of the near presence of God
Himself in their midst in all His holiness and power and love.

He faced them quite suddenly with a challenge to trust Him
to take them out of their depths in a great act of faith and
obedience. *"And when he had ceased speaking, he said to Simon,
'Put out into the deep and let down your nets for a catch'."* At this
moment Jesus risked Simon's friendship and loyalty. It was
an abrupt and difficult challenge. There was a huge crowd of
staring onlookers. They had fished all night and taken nothing.
It was a ridiculous act, to throw in their nets at midday in the
way Jesus was commanding them. This was a crucial test as
to how far he was now prepared to trust in the mere word of
Jesus when it made nonsense of everything his experience of
life had taught him, and how far he was prepared to go in
obeying the command of Jesus when he did not understand.

The important point for us to notice is that Jesus, who up
to this moment had shown so much tact in His approach to
Simon was not afraid so soon to change His tactics and so
abruptly to haul His man right out of his depths and face him
with a world of mystery and faith. Moreover when the miracle
happened and *"they enclosed a great shoal of fish and . . . their nets
were breaking,"* Peter felt that in this world of mystery and faith
into which Jesus had begun to launch him, all the foundations
of his hitherto secure life were completely knocked away. He
found himself not only beyond his depth, but completely sub-
merged in self-abasement and utterly oppressed by the sense

he now had of the holiness of this Jesus, in whose presence there had come to him this terrible challenge to probe a new world of fearful dimensions and depths. *"But when Simon Peter saw it, he fell down at Jesus' knees, saying, 'Depart from me, for I am a sinful man, O Lord'."* In the presence of this Jesus who had seemed so kind and familiar Peter now found himself *"astonished"* in the midst of a new world of mystery and holiness and love.

It was not because Peter had just committed some one particular sin, the memory of which had now come back to sear his conscience, that he now uttered this abject confession of his guiltiness. Peter had always been a decent fellow, with high aims and a fair record of honest living. But in the presence of Jesus he simply finds this sudden overwhelming sense of his creaturely weakness, and the unworthiness of his whole being and nature, coming upon him, and he can no longer find any comfort or sense in dividing his life into good parts and bad parts. He is from now on, in everything he does or says or thinks, a *"sinful man"* bowing at the feet of divine holiness and mercy in Jesus Christ. He must always judge himself now in the light of the glory and holiness of the new world he has become conscious of in Jesus Christ.

All this can still take place within the Church today. When a man is confronted by Jesus Christ in the Gospel and Sacraments within the Church, he is still confronted by this same world of fearful new dimensions and depths that so awed Peter as he bowed before Jesus. He is still confronted by a tremendous challenge to faith and obedience and utter self-surrender towards Jesus. He is confronted by the same mystery, the same holiness, and the same jealous and loving claim for absolute loyalty and love as brought Peter down on his face in the boat that day. What Jesus did to Peter He still wants to do for men and women in the Church today.

We must allow this to happen in the Church today to all who come into our midst for fellowship and friendship and worship. It is true that we must always be human and friendly in the Church, and must seek to attract men into our midst on a familiar basis, as Christ did. But we must never allow them to remain too long at their ease as they are. Very soon we must challenge them to launch out with us into this world of mystery that is there in Christ, and that can be entered only by an act of faith which demands the surrender of our own human reasoning. We must confront them with the blazing holiness that there is in Christ so that they too will fall at His feet and cry, *"Depart from me, for I am a sinful man, O Lord."* We must confront them with the whole demand of this living Christ for the worship and devotion of all their mind and heart and soul and strength. Until we challenge them in this way we are not fulfilling the purpose for which Christ has sent us to them and we are merely playing with men instead of making disciples of them.

What kind of a Christ are we to present to men in our preaching and teaching? Certainly there is in the New Testament a picture of Jesus in the aspect of familiar human friendship in which He first approached the fishermen by the lake. But there is also in the New Testament a clear and vivid picture of the exalted glorious Lord, of whose true being John caught a glimpse on the Lord's day in the Isle of Patmos. "One like a son of man, clothed with a long robe and with a golden girdle round his breast; his head and his hair were white as white wool, white as snow; his eyes were like a flame of fire, his feet were like burnished bronze refined as in a furnace, and his voice was like the sound of many waters; in his right hand he held seven stars, from his mouth issued a sharp two-edged sword, and his face was like the sun shining in full strength. When I saw him, I fell at his feet as though dead" (Rev. I. 13–17). The Christ before whose feet John fell was not a different being from the Jesus in the boat before whom Peter fell. There are not two Christs here to choose between, but only one Jesus Christ who is both the human being, interested in fishing and asking favours of His friends, and also the holy Lord who unites in His person God and man, Heaven and earth, and who brings near the mystery of the Kingdom of God so that men can launch into the depths as they enter His friendship and get to know Him better. This is the mystery which Peter began to realise in a dim way that day on the lake. And in the Church today we must be careful never to cancel out one aspect of Christ by overemphasising the other aspect. If we do this we distort Him. Certainly we must present Jesus the human Friend. But we must present Him also as Lord and God.

We must not cover over the burning holiness that shattered Peter and John. If we speak only of the humanity that drew men into Jesus's friendship on a first meeting, and remain silent about the depths of mystery and holiness in the person of Jesus we prevent men from entering the greatest privilege that life can offer them, for it is only by launching out into these depths that they can come to have real faith at last, and can come to know who God is, and what sin and its forgiveness really mean. It is tragic that we are often so careful to keep men in the shallows by trying to present a Christianity that is too reasonable and "simple."

The Absolution and Promise heard in the Depths

As Peter fell at Jesus's feet in the boat he was conscious of being faced not only with a holiness that condemned him, but also by a forgiving love that found expression in a word of assurance and promise. *"And Jesus said to Simon, 'Do not be afraid; henceforth you will be catching men'."* Such forgiving love must already have had something to do with bringing Peter down on his knees, for no vision of mere majestic holiness could have so utterly broken him.

" 'Do not be afraid; henceforth you will be catching men'." To be forgiven by Christ is an experience in which we not only know that the past is blotted out but that the future is guaranteed, because, from now on, life is to be lived on a new basis of friendship and trust towards God. The future for Peter in that moment in the boat was filled with promise, with a vision of a life of usefulness and an eternity of glory. It is the same for each of us. Whatever be our sphere of service or our circumstances, He trusts us, in spite of our past, and says to each of us, "Fear not, you are going to be my servant, and I am going to make your life fruitful and worth while." But to whom does He say this kind of thing? To those who have been in the depths, and who have so completely lost their self-confidence that they cannot even stand upon their own feet again unless they hear a word like this.

There is, in this word of Jesus, also a promise of success and fruitfulness even in the most unlikely circumstances. That day Jesus had shown Peter where to put down the net. Under most unlikely circumstances there had been this overwhelming catch. This was a sign that Peter, the fisherman for Christ, would not fail in the task for which Jesus had called him. The miracle which Jesus had just done was for Peter a promise and foretaste of how Jesus was going to guide and direct his fishing for men in the sea of this world's life, and of how marvellous the results of his efforts were to be. We can remember how gloriously Jesus began to fulfil this promise when, on the day of Pentecost, Peter went out and preached, and the Holy Ghost worked, men's minds were opened and their hearts were moved, and three thousand were added to the Church. Peter had good reason to remember this incident all his days, for he had to face difficulties, discouragement and failure too. Whenever Christ sent him and commanded him to put down the net, even where fishing seemed in vain, he must obey, he must believe, for the promise of the Lord had been given to him not only in words but in the marvellous catch on the lake that day.

Have we not this same promise? Are we not all together commissioned to continue in our generation the same work of gathering, into the net of Christ's love, men of all nations and kindreds and tongues? Let us never hold back or doubt or despair. Even though the time does not seem to be the right time, even though the place does not seem to be the right place, even though the opportunity seems to be restricted and the difficulties many, if we put out at His word, He will indeed fulfil His promise.

THE HEALING OF SIMON'S
MOTHER-IN-LAW

And immediately he left the synagogue, and entered the house of
Simon and Andrew, with James and John. Now Simon's mother-in-
law lay sick with a fever, and immediately they told him of her.
And he came and took her by the hand and lifted her up, and the
fever left her; and she served them.

Mk. 1. 29–31.

CHRIST IN A COMMONPLACE SETTING

*"And immediately he left the synagogue, and entered the house of
Simon and Andrew, with James and John."*

This all took place at home on the Sabbath day immediately
after the Church service was over. Something quite memorable
and unusual had taken place during the service. Jesus had
proved His power in the synagogue at the hour of public
worship. He had made a spectacular change come about in a
mad-man by casting the devil out of him. There had been a
good deal of stir and a good deal of talk.

We are not surprised to read about this in the Gospels, for
today when we come together to worship Him in the Church,
Jesus still comes to meet us with power to cast out the satanic
disorders and unruly passions and desires that make our life
in the world so bitter and wretched for ourselves and others
around us. In generation after generation Jesus has indeed
proved Himself the One who is able to deal with the devils
in the heart of men at public worship. So much is this true
that we have come to imagine that the Church or synagogue is
the peculiar and appropriate setting for Jesus Christ to work in,
and we are apt to think of Him as One who is so absorbed there
that He has little time and care to be anywhere else on earth.
We imagine that Jesus is most at home within an ecclesiastical
setting.

But now in the story of this miracle we see Him coming out
of this ecclesiastical setting right into the midst of ordinary
human life, out of the sanctuary into the living-room, out of

the place of quiet and holy solemnity into the place of bustle and tears and laughter, out of the place of worship into the place where we cook and eat dinners. How will He behave now? It is good to know that Jesus has brought into the world a power that enables Him to do mighty works within the Church building down the road, but what can it do here? It is good to know that Jesus Christ can offer us a faith to make troubled people pious and submissive within the synagogue, but can He also offer a faith to make people serve another in love and humility in the midst of their concrete earthly situations of human need? Can the Lord who has overcome the devils in the synagogue on the Sabbath day also deal with the fevers and frets that seize men and women in the home and business world? Here in the home is the place where for many of us the real test begins. Can the power of Jesus stand up to this test?

The home into which Jesus was taken after the service that Sabbath in Capernaum was very ordinary. Perhaps the fact that Simon's wife's mother, and also Andrew his brother lived in the same house as Simon and his wife means that all the problems that face people today through overcrowding were also present there too. It is good also to remember that Simon and Andrew his brother, when they followed Jesus, did not enter a monastic order, but held on to the responsibility of owning their own property, calculating their own expenses and managing their own household affairs, and they brought Jesus into the midst of all this.

Jesus, on His visit to this ordinary home, proved, as He did again on many occasions, that this very place is as true and fitting a setting for His divine work and ministry as was the synagogue. Should we not expect this? After all, when He came into the world it was a very humble cottage home at Nazareth that He chose as the place where He was to spend His infancy and childhood. Many of the men and women He chose as His friends and companions were also quite ordinary people immersed in the everyday problems of life. We must realise the profound significance of these facts. They mean that we do not need to leave Jesus Christ behind when we leave Church on Sundays and are confronted by all the ordinary things that make up home and business life with all its petty, technical, and not very inspiring, details. He is able and willing to be with us at the dinner table, an hour after we have left the "Lord's Table."

CHRIST AND THE COMMONPLACE FEVER

"Now Simon's mother-in-law lay sick with a fever."

Certain of the diseases and disabilities which Jesus cured make us very naturally think of certain of the moral and spiritual diseases and infirmities which spoil our individual and social lives. When we read in the Gospels of Jesus curing blindness, it is natural for us to think also of how He can cure the blindness that affects our souls and minds, and prevents us from grasping the reality of the new spiritual world that He has brought into our midst in all its hidden glory. When we read of His raising the dead, we likewise think of the fact that our souls are as dead as any lifeless corpse till Jesus Himself comes to us to raise us up to share His own life. When we read of His cleansing the leper, we think of the filth and defilement that can destroy and isolate the human soul in hopeless misery, till He comes to touch it and cleanse and renew it. So when we follow Jesus to this home, and see Him lay His hand upon Simon's wife's mother to cure her fever, we naturally think of the moral and spiritual fevers that possess the minds and hearts of men today, and make us impotent and useless until He comes to lay His hand upon them to still them.

Life today for multitudes of men and women can become a feverish affair. Evil desires, if we allow them scope, can become fevers raising the temperature of our life to an unhealthy level, sickening our souls and sapping our moral powers. The craving to revenge ourselves on those who have wronged us, can consume us like any other fever. Our natural and right desires, too, can become fevers when we allow them to become too strong and dominant. Thus even our love of amusement or sport can rise to the pitch of a fever that is a real sickness of soul. There are gambling fevers and stock-exchange fevers and collectors' fevers, so strong and uncontrollable that men need to be saved from them. Life can also be made feverish through the mere frictions and tensions in which we are involved by living with other people.

"And immediately they told him of her."

Do we see the connexion between such fevers and Jesus

Christ? Do we really believe that He can lay His hand upon such things and cure them? Perhaps even the disciples had difficulty in seeing the connexion between His divine power and this common everyday complaint. After all, there was nothing desperate in this case. It was neither a mortal nor a permanently disabling sickness. After a day or two in bed she would be all right again. Why then expect the Lord specially to trouble Himself over such a complaint? But they at least asked Him about it.

"Immediately they told him of her. And he came and took her by the hand and lifted her up, and the fever left her."

We have to realise that Jesus seeks to cure not only the mortal sicknesses that threaten our eternal blessedness, but also those everyday ailments that are more upsetting than they are dangerous—and yet are dangerous because they are upsetting. It is a great matter for us to be able to confess with assurance that Christ has saved us from the power of Death and Hell. It is a great matter to have put Him to the test in the crises of life when we have felt ourselves so involved in trouble and so desperate that there could have been no other refuge but in Him. There is, however, a further step that some of us have to take. That is simply to discover that we can go to Him with our feverish passions and pride, with our covetous desires and foolish tempers, even when they are at their height, and have them cured even in a moment by His marvellous power. For the cure in this instance was complete in one moment. He took her by the hand and the fever left her. There was no slow convalescence and no enfeebling after-effects.

We must not try to keep Jesus Christ in reserve for days of utter and inescapable crisis. He wants to be of service to us also in the midst of our everyday needs and worries and fevers. He wants us to stretch out a hand to touch Him in the midst of life's "throng and press" in order that we may become instantly "whole again." As a symbol of this desire of His, Jesus one day washed the disciples' feet, cleansing them from the dust of the days' journey. Peter did not like seeing Jesus stoop to such a little and menial task for him. His pride rebelled and he protested. But when Jesus assured him that he needed such cleansing, Peter said, "Lord, not my feet only, but also my hands and my head." Jesus replied, "He who has bathed does not need to wash, except for his feet, but he is clean all over" (Jn. XIII. 1–11). The meaning of Jesus's remark is clear. Many of us, like Peter, have been bathed by Jesus. We have received His once-for-all cleansing and salvation from the guilt of sin, the threat of Death and Hell, and the power of evil and darkness, and we have no more fear of these things. But as we walk on our life's daily journey, our feet become dirty again, and He wants to serve us by constantly washing our feet in the fever, heat and dirt of the ordinary day. It is tragic that we who profess to be Christians sing His praise for saving us from Hell, and yet allow many of our sicknesses of soul, which could be checked by His mighty power, to take their otherwise inevitable course and rise to a hectic pitch, thus spoiling not only our own peace and stability, but also our Christian witness and service.

CHRIST AND THE COMMONPLACE TASK

"And she served them."

She did not first go to the temple to sing praise, though her soul may have felt like doing so. The situation that faced her called rather for an act of immediate service than for poetry or rapturous song. She got down to it, and did the commonplace job of work.

Jesus Himself sat amongst those she ministered to. Here is another wonderful characteristic of His grace. Half an hour before this she was lying there helpless and useless, and He came and ministered graciously to her. Now He sits down at the table amongst the rest of them, and allows her to return His kindness by ministering to Him in this material and commonplace way. He graciously puts Himself in the position of being able to accept her humble service. Here indeed He shows Himself at the height of His wonderful love and humility towards us. He comes not only to cure us and save us, but also to allow us to minister to Him as if He needed us. He is willing to inspire and accept the tasks we have to do in our daily life, as if our whole life, even in its lowliest aspects were a glorious service of Himself. After we have allowed Him to deal with our fever, it will not be long before we find confronting us an opportunity, perhaps of humble service, and if we are willing to stoop to the task we will find that it is not only our fellow men we are serving, but that Christ is there too, Christ perhaps in the guise of a needy lonely fellow being, even begging help and accepting it gladly and graciously when it is given. The story of this woman pouring out her new found strength of body and soul into the task that Christ was there to inspire, is a type of the true Christian life which He wants to see us living. Here is a true expression of Christian sanctity.

"Immediately" is the word St. Luke adds about her service of Jesus. "And immediately she rose and served them" (Lk. iv. 39).

She lost no time, for the challenge of the task did not allow her to do so. Christ, as we have seen, does not want to be held in reserve. But neither does He want us to hold ourselves in reserve in face of the task that "immediately" faces us, whatever that may be. There are future tasks for us in the service of Christ which we can hold before our imagination and dream of accomplishing for Him some day when we have had more experience, more maturity, more training in His school. But often the situation we are involved in calls for immediate action. We find ourselves like Peter's mother-in-law in a key position in the centre of a situation in which someone must start taking action—with the power of Christ abundantly at our disposal. Why then need we wait too long? Christ does indeed inspire the distant task. He bids some of us to lift up our eyes (Jn. iv. 35) over the whole field of this world's life, to see what task may call us to foresake home and leave our settled ways. But we must not let our dreams about the glory of this distant task blind us to the fact that for all of us there is also the immediate task crying out for our much more humble and commonplace exercise of His divine strength. What of Simon's wife's mother? It is possible that as years passed she became one of the "widows" and deaconesses who held an important place in the life of the early Church. She may have also been given some place in furthering the mission of the Church as it spread all over Palestine and then over Asia Minor. But these were as yet distant tasks. How could she sincerely have taken these up later on, unless she had first of all faced the immediate and commonplace task in the midst of which He who had served her, was there waiting now for her to serve Him and His people?

THE CLEANSING OF THE LEPER

And a leper came to him beseeching him, and kneeling said to him, "If you will, you can make me clean." Moved with pity, he stretched out his hand and touched him, and said to him, "I will; be clean." And immediately the leprosy left him, and he was made clean. And he sternly charged him, and sent him away at once, and said to him, "See that you say nothing to any one; but go, show yourself to the priest, and offer for your cleansing what Moses commanded, for a proof to the people." But he went out and began to talk freely about it, and to spread the news, so that Jesus could no longer openly enter a town, but was out in the country; and people came to him from every quarter.

Mk. 1. 40–5.

To contract leprosy was regarded as the most cruel and terrible fate that could come to any man in that ancient world. It was better to be dead than to be a leper. He came under Old Testament laws that made him an outcast, cut off from all normal contact with healthy society, compelled to live apart from wife and children, forced to tear his clothes and wear a white shroud that already proclaimed him a living corpse to be shunned by all who were healthy. Wherever he moved he had to cry, "Unclean, unclean," to warn the rest of mankind away from him.

We need not wonder that such laws were rigidly kept. On a visit to a small leper colony in Palestine, some years ago, I was taken, along with others, to the room of a leper who, we were told, was dying of the disease. We looked at the poor fellow on his bed, wasted away in body yet still living, beyond cure and almost beyond recognition as a human being, except that his eyes as they looked at ours seemed to reproach us for standing so far away. One could understand why, in the days when leprosy was an incurable and widespread scourge, men were so afraid of contracting it that they forced the leper to live and work and die apart from the rest of the community.

Their loneliness under this cruelty was a terrible burden. But if a leper had any sense of God at all there was an even harder burden. It was in the name of God that they were condemned to this terrible separation. The leper was condemned to his lot by the word and decree of God's priests acting in God's name. And leprosy had come to be regarded as a special sign of God's displeasure. Most other diseases were called sicknesses. Leprosy was called uncleanness, and its worst consequence to the man who believed in God was that it cut him off from all normal contact with the temple, its services and its fellowship—the place where God came to meet His people.

Such, then, was the despair of heart, mind and soul, and the bitterness that were the lot of the leper in these days. We can try to imagine what this terrible isolation, this sense of guilt and uncleanness, meant for him. Perhaps it is not too difficult for some of us to do this, for we have people today who count themselves as lepers in the midst of our society. There is no sign of physical leprosy on their bodies. They mix with society to an extent, and outwardly live fairly normal lives. Yet they suffer from such an unrelievable sense of moral uncleanness that the only description of their state that they feel to fit them is simply that of moral leprosy. For a few of them this sense of intense uncleanness produces mental illness. It can keep some mistakenly from coming near the Church. But it drives others into the Church, always with the prayer in their heart that the grace of God will make them clean in heart again. Perhaps such are not far from the Kingdom of God. If there was hope for the leper in Palestine, there is hope for them. And though this sense of being a moral leper is not a normal state with all of us, it certainly overtakes many of us at times. What healthy Christian man who looks at Jesus Christ in all His love and holiness does not feel, especially as he approaches the Lord's table, that he is indeed little else but a leper in his filth and defilement of heart and soul?

Therefore this story is not simply about one leper whom Jesus cured in Palestine, but about every one of us.

There are three miracles in this one story. It is difficult to decide which is the greatest of them.

THE MIRACLE OF FAITH

This man's mind might have remained utterly broken under the consequences of his leprosy. He might have accepted his lot as inevitable, prepared for a lingering, lonely death, and adapted his whole outlook and way of living to this end. That is what leprosy did for many lepers in Palestine. They settled down with other lepers, accepted their fate and did not dare even to think of breaking the age-long traditions and laws that kept them for ever apart from the rest of mankind. And in their isolation they nourished despair and bitterness and mistrust of God and man in their hearts.

But not so our friend this leper. He refused to sit down with the others in their gloom. He refused to sulk or despair. He had hope. He was prepared to break through all the rigid conventions that had kept lepers so utterly apart if he could find good reason. And he found his good reason. Perhaps he found it through the Scriptures. He remembered how the Old Testament spoke of the cleansing and restoration of lepers. There must be hope. He remembered the story of how some lepers were the first to enjoy the blessings of God's deliverance in the relief of Samaria. He remembered how one of the prophets, a man of God, Elisha, had cleansed Naaman the leper in the Jordan. The power of God was great enough. And then he heard of Jesus, the man of God. He was going about doing all the wonderful things that men like Elijah and Elisha had done centuries before. Some people said He did this to show He was the great prophet, the Messiah of His people. He would go to Him. It did not matter that He was always surrounded by crowds who hated lepers and stoned them away. If the Syrian Naaman went to Elisha why should he himself not be allowed to go to Jesus of Nazareth? He went to Him, "*beseeching him, and kneeling said to him, 'If you will, you can make me clean'.*" For Him to do this meant the violation of the law of leprosy, the breaking through of strong and binding rules. No doubt there was consternation among the crowd round Jesus who scattered when this man approached. But his faith was miraculously strong enough to do such violence to the conventions and settled ways that sealed the doom of his fellow lepers.

Jesus expected faith to do this kind of thing when it appeared in men's hearts. He once affirmed that in His own days the Kingdom of God had "suffered violence," and, He went on to say "men of violence take it by force." (Mt. xi. 12.) Was He not thinking of men like this leper? Who were the men in His day who won the privileges and powers of the Kingdom? They were those who were prepared to do violence to all kinds of things that tied them down and prevented them from coming to Christ and receiving His blessing. This call of Christ to us to become "men of violence" is a challenge to us to be prepared to do violence to our own prejudices and fixed habits of thought and behaviour, to be prepared to break forcibly out of the routine and the grooves in which our lives have hitherto been lived, and to be prepared to do the surprising and unconventional things that might scandalise those who hold to rigid conventions. We, too, like this leper should look at Christ afresh and listen anew to His word till we too are inspired to a new degree of discontent with our settled ways, our pessimism and our despairing mental habits, to a new impatience with the social and ecclesiastical conventions that keep us back from going into fresh avenues of Christian experience and service, and to a new boldness before men.

The violent and miraculous faith of this leper was inspired by his vision of the glory and power of Jesus. "*If you will, you can make me clean.*" Who is He? He is the One who can deal with all the problems that revolve round this terrible sense of uncleanness that blights human life today, that cuts so many souls off in isolation, that paralyses human usefulness, that drives to despair and sometimes to suicide. When we look at Jesus we can see many glorious and appealing aspects of His person. He is the One who can grip the young and become their hero. He is the One who can bring the nations together as the Prince of Peace. He is the One who can give rest and comfort to the weary and heavy laden. But for many the first and most wonderful aspect of His glory will be, that He is the One who can make men clean, blotting out the guilt of the past, removing all defilement of soul and spirit, and making us fit for full and healthy fellowship with God and with man.

THE MIRACLE OF LOVE

As this man broke into the Kingdom of God through the violence of his faith, a miracle of love met him on the threshold.

"*Moved with pity,*" Jesus "*stretched out his hand and touched him, and said to him, 'I will; be clean'.*"

Jesus touched him. Think of what this touch meant. It meant that for the first time in his diseased life this lonely man felt that sympathy and love were at last reaching him again—not just from man but from One who was the bearer of God's grace and cleansing power. It meant that this leper knew that now he was not alone in his desperate seeking to break through all the barriers and restraints that condemned the lepers so terribly, for here was One who had broken through from God's side of the barrier to meet him and save him. It was a touch so sympathetic as to assure him beyond all doubt that this man Jesus, with all His cleansing power and holiness and love, could really enter the agony of the leper's condition, could feel Himself the constant horror of this sense of uncleanness which took away all the meaning from life, could understand the gnawing heartbreak of the social outcaste. Even with all his defilement he was now in touch with divine holiness as well as love, and he was not consumed or struck dead. He had begun to disbelieve that true human pity and compassion existed anywhere. He had come towards even Jesus with some doubt about this clouding his mind. "*If you will,*" he had said, "*You can make me clean.*" But the doubts he had expressed had now all been driven away. He found that a true human feeling of pity and compassion were here in this man, who now so strangely represented God Himself.

Jesus touched the leper, and His touch made everything different. Do we realise that today He touches us in the same way? The Sacraments, Baptism and the Lord's Supper, are the means whereby He really touches us today. They are His own special signs, as His touch was to the leper, that He deals with us not just through ideas flashed on our minds, or words thrown at us from a safe distance, but as One who lays His hand in self-identifying love on all the worst spots of our terrible condition and need. They remind us that as He the Son of God united Himself with our human flesh and took on Himself all our sicknesses and diseases in His incarnation, so today He seeks in a no less real way to unite us to Himself and to bring His glorious life and holiness compassion and to bear with real and living cleansing power on everything we are and do and say. The Sacraments tell us that He has become flesh of our leprous flesh, in order that we might become flesh of His glorious and perfect heavenly body.

And yet we can remain unaware of the meaning of this self-identifying touch of Jesus Christ upon our life in all its aspects. We nurse our worries and anxieties in isolation from Him even though all the time He wants us to know the power of His staying and supporting hand, His willingness to share our troubles with us. We nurse our sense of guilt apart. We allow our unconfessed sins and moral sores to fester away in their dark hiding-places, when all the time, if we would bring them into the light of His presence, His cleansing touch would cure us and liberate us for ever from them. The result is that we think the Christian faith is irrelevant. We feel that it doesn't seem to touch either us, or modern life. We feel that it doesn't touch us at work or at our leisure or in our culture. But Christ's hand is always stretched out towards us in power and pity and grace, in order to make His Gospel relevant to us in the midst of our complex, bewildering, fast and lonely life. If, in face of this, Christianity continues to seem irrelevant to us, that is simply because we are not allowing Christ to touch us. Most of us will neither break through our modern conventions by faith and come to Him, nor in our pride will we let Him treat us as if we required cleansing. And the worst tragedy of all is that some of us have listened so little to His words and looked so little in His face that we still think He is too holy, too good, too high and mighty ever to come near to us. Yet his hand is stretched out to touch us whatever our state or need. This is the miracle of love that meets any man, however much a leper, who will enter the Kingdom of heaven—and it meets him even before he has crossed the threshold of that Kingdom.

THE MIRACLE OF POWER

Jesus stretched out His hand and touched him, *"and immediately the leprosy left him, and he was made clean."*

Leprosy was regarded as the most infectious and putrefying disease. It was because all men were afraid of its contagious power that they were afraid to touch the leper. It was known to be more powerful to defile than any known medicine was to cleanse. But Jesus was not afraid to touch the leper because He had with Him and in Himself a power and blessed influence that was more mighty to cleanse than anything else on earth was to defile. Therefore in contact with Himself all the polluted currents of this world's life could be purified and all its evil infections washed away, without His own power and purity in any way being diminished. When the Son of God became a man He took upon Himself our human flesh, in its fallen and weak condition and subject even to death, but in the midst of all the temptation, the filth and defilement, sordidness and contact with sin, that this closest of all unions with our human flesh involved Him in, He, Himself, neither in His divine nor human nature suffered any defilement but sanctified everything He was allowed to touch, and judged and condemned everything that would not submit to His touch.

This is a fact from which we must take real encouragement in our work for the Church today. Nothing tends to depress or discourage us more than the seeming power of evil influence to defile young and hopeful lives, to infect homes, to turn happiness into bitterness, to pollute even our Churches so that Jesus Christ is given a bad name. We put out our efforts to train and influence and win our young people for Christ. We pray and expend our labour over them. But we are often beaten because evil in this world is so powerful and infectious a force that we begin to ask ourselves, which is the stronger power today? The power of Christ to cleanse and save or the power of evil to pollute and destroy?

This miracle gives us the assurance that such a question is foolish, and that all our gloomy suspicions on this matter are false. Before Christ's sanctifying and cleansing touch evil must always lose its grip and give place to the new creative power of His glorious Kingdom. No matter how closely we are involved in our daily contact with things that can defile us if we give way to them, nevertheless our minds and wills can be kept cleansed and renewed from day to day if we will let Him ever speak His fresh word of cleansing to us within the life of the Church, and touch us afresh through the gracious ministry of His Sacraments. Our failure to counteract the influence of evil in this world and in the Church is always due, not to our lack of a sufficient power to cleanse our environment, but rather to our failure to let Him really touch us, and through us to touch and cleanse what we too have to touch and influence in His name.

THE HEALING OF THE PARALYTIC

And when he returned to Capernaum after some days, it was reported that he was at home. And many were gathered together, so that there was no longer room for them, not even about the door; and he was preaching the word to them. And they came, bringing to him a paralytic carried by four men. And when they could not get near him because of the crowd, they removed the roof above him; and when they had made an opening, they let down the pallet on which the paralytic lay. And when Jesus saw their faith, he said to the paralytic, "My son, your sins are forgiven." Now some of the scribes were sitting there, questioning in their hearts, "Why does this man speak thus? It is blasphemy! Who can forgive sins but God alone?" And immediately Jesus, perceiving in his spirit that they thus questioned within themselves, said to them, "Why do you question thus in your hearts? Which is easier, to say to the paralytic, 'Your sins are forgiven,' or to say, 'Rise, take up your pallet and walk?' But that you may know that the Son of man has authority on earth to forgive sins"—he said to the paralytic—"I say to you, rise, take up your pallet and go home." And he rose, and immediately took up the pallet and went out before them all; so that they were all amazed and glorified God saying, "We never saw anything like this!"

Mk. II. 1–12.

THE GOOD NEWS

The greatest of the Old Testament prophets, in their moments of highest and clearest vision describe the day of the Kingdom of God as a day when men will enjoy, as the first and greatest gift of God, the forgiveness of their sins. "Behold," writes Jeremiah, "the days are coming, says the Lord, when I will make a new covenant with the house of Israel and the house of Judah. . . . This is the covenant which I will make with the house of Israel after these days, says the Lord: I will put my law within them, and I will write it upon their hearts; and I will be their God, and they shall be my people. And no longer shall each man teach his neighbour and each his brother, saying, 'Know the Lord,' for they shall all know me, from the least of them to the greatest, says the Lord; and I will forgive their iniquity, and I will remember their sin no more" (Jer. XXXI. 31–35).

22

The last half of the book of Isaiah repeats the same glorious news in poetry. There the prophet talks about a "new thing" that God was beginning to do for His people and for all men. The "new thing" was this:

> I, I am He
> who blots out your transgressions
>   for my own sake
> and I will not remember your sins.
>
> (Is. XLIII. 25)

This "new thing" is to be fully fulfilled in the glorious days when the Messiah will come.

These were the passages Jesus had in mind in the first sermon He ever preached when He made His great announcement, "The time is fulfilled, and the Kingdom of God is at hand; repent, and believe the Gospel." This was indeed great and exciting news: that the day had now come when men can enjoy the liberating power of the forgiveness of sins.

But many of His hearers had different ideas of what was to happen when the Messiah brought in the Kingdom of God. Some thought it would mean a new era of political freedom for the Jewish nation. Some thought that they would see ominous signs of the end of the world and of coming judgment in the moon and sun and stars. One of the most widely debated, and highly debatable questions of the day was: what can we expect to see taking place on this earth when the Kingdom really comes? What exactly will the coming of the Kingdom mean?

Jesus gave a clear answer to this question when He healed this paralytic man early in His ministry. It was an important occasion. "Pharisees and teachers of the law" (Lk. v. 17) had come together from every part of the country and Jerusalem to find out what His teaching and work really meant, and huge crowds had congregated to watch Him and listen. Four men, after great trouble, had managed to lay in front of Him their friend, a man hopelessly and pathetically paralysed lying on his mattress. Many were curious. Many of them eagerly expected to hear Him speak the Word of the Kingdom that would make this lame man leap up like a young deer in fulfilment of Isaiah's prophecy, "Then shall the lame man leap like a hart" (Is.

xxxv. 6). This was their idea of what the Kingdom of God should mean there and then.

But Jesus forced them to think again. He looked down pityingly on the poor fellow at His feet, and the first thing He said, quite deliberately, was, "*My son, your sins are forgiven.*" Having said this He, again, deliberately, paused. There is no mistaking His meaning. The coming of the Kingdom of God meant above everything else that the new day of plentiful and free forgiveness had dawned for this earth. "*The Son of man has authority on earth to forgive sins.*"

The Disappointed Onlookers

To anyone who really understood what it meant, Jesus's announcement that He had come first of all to forgive sins should have immediately brought rejoicing and wonder. It meant, as we have seen, that a new age had indeed dawned for this earth. It meant the beginning of an entirely new and close relationship between God and His people.

Certainly, already in Old Testament times men had had some experience of their sins being forgiven. Those who attended the annual ceremonies on the Day of Atonement in the Temple must have felt even in a dim and distant way that God had cleansed them from sin, and many of the Psalms in the Old Testament reflect such feelings. But such experiences were not deep enough for it to be said that the new day of God's nearness in forgiving love had yet dawned. For that, men must still wait till the day of the Kingdom of God. But now this day had come. Here was the Messiah Himself announcing it, "Your sins are forgiven."

Yet Jesus's audience did not understand the tremendous significance of His words, and many in the friendly crowd were disappointed. They expected something more outwardly exciting. They had read in their Old Testament:

> Then the eyes of the blind shall be opened
> and the ears of the deaf unstopped;
> then shall the lame man leap like a hart,
> and the tongue of the dumb sing for joy.

(Is. xxxv. 5–6)

And they shall beat their swords into plowshares,
        and their spears into pruning hooks;
nation shall not lift up sword against nation,
        neither shall they learn war any more;
but they shall sit every man under his vine and
                                under his fig tree,
        and none shall make them afraid.

(Mic. IV. 3–4)

No more want! No more tyranny! No more disease! If the Kingdom of God had really come, this was what they expected first of all: health and wealth and security and happiness for all. Let Jesus now fulfil these their Old Testament visions of bliss and plenty! The four men who had gone to so much trouble to bring their friend to Jesus, must have betrayed a little impatience when, instead, they heard as His first word, "*Your sins are forgiven.*" They were disappointed with the order of things in His "Kingdom of God."

We, who live today, suffer the same disappointment with the order of things in the Kingdom as it is preached today. We tend always to feel that the most urgent problems in human life are our material problems. The people we have to speak to in Jesus's name, suffer not only from sin but from social injustices, from bad housing, from unreasonable and cruel diseases, from material poverty and distress. There is, moreover, the threat hanging over our whole world of an atomic war in which all the wealth of our great cultural heritage and scientific discovery will be wiped out, and only a small portion of the human race on earth has the possibility of surviving.

We would like to be able to proclaim to men in the name of Jesus the real possibility of miraculous recovery from all kinds of otherwise incurable diseases. We would like to be able to announce in His name a social programme that will remove all slums and economic injustice, the abolition of the possibility of war and, indeed, the abolition of death itself. It would be wonderful indeed if we could speak such a word in the name of Christ to the men and women of today who are eagerly looking to us to give them some hope for the fulfilment here and now on earth of the glorious material dreams and visions of the old prophets of Israel.

But Jesus deliberately suspended such hopes in the hearts of men of His own day. He always put the salvation of the soul from sin and guilt before the redemption of the body from illness and bondage. This was why He answered the temptation to make the stones bread in the wilderness with the words, "Man shall not live by bread alone, but by every word that proceeds from the mouth of God" (Mt. iv. 4) thus committing Himself to a ministry in which He would put the solution of man's material problems in its true place in God's order of things, and not in the first place. This was why He uttered words of warning to those who wanted to save and care for the earthly state of the body before the salvation of the soul from sin and guilt. "And do not fear those who kill the body but cannot kill the soul; rather fear him who can destroy both soul and body in hell" (Mt. x. 28). "For what does it profit a man, to gain the whole world and forfeit his life?" (Mk. viii. 36).

It is true that Jesus healed men's bodies and showed real, deep and compassionate concern for the material well-being of those around Him. But at the same time He disappointed men of His time by not doing His healings on a wide and wholesale enough scale for them to be able to claim that their great material hopes of the Kingdom were fulfilled. John the Baptist who began with great hopes of seeing Jesus bring in the Kingdom was so disappointed with the meagre material results of Jesus's early ministry that he sent messengers from his prison to Jesus with the question "Are you he who is to come, or shall we look for another?" (Mt. xi. 3). Jesus never put the healing of the body or the solution of earth's material problems first on His programme.

To Jesus the Kingdom of God had to come in two distinct stages: First of all the coming near of the Kingdom of God must mean the proclamation and acceptance of the forgiveness of sins. After this has been done men must wait on the good pleasure of God for the day or the hour in which He will fulfil the further promise of complete healing, of the redemption of the bodies of men from corruption and death, and the bringing in of lasting human happiness and prosperity.

The message which we preach today in the name of Jesus has not changed. The Kingdom of God is here in our midst today in the same way as it was in the time of Jesus. It is here in such a way that we can proclaim to men here and now the word that means immediate release from the burden of the guilty past, the healing of the wounded conscience, and the removal of the fear of the judgment seat of God. But it is not yet in our midst in such a way that we can proclaim immediate release from the burden and pains of earth's sicknesses and warfares, and from physical death. To the men and women today who are so eagerly looking to us to give them some hope for the fulfilment of the visions of the old prophets of Israel the only word we can speak with certainty is the same word which Jesus spoke to this paralytic man in His day, "*Your sins are forgiven.*"

This does not mean that we do not need to care about, or travail over, these other material problems that so paralyse men's lives and hamper their service of God—sickness and housing and want and war. We must have a word for men in the name of Christ that will help them to make their decision about such problems, and, indeed, overcome in the midst of such problems. Christ not only had compassion on the sick but as we shall see He sealed His word of forgiveness with miracles of healing as a sign that not only the souls, but also the bodies of men must be cared for and redeemed. He surely wants to help us to overcome as far as can be done the diseases and material evils that hamper good living or destroy men's lives today. But, for the word which will finally abolish all these problems, men will have to wait till He comes again in the day of the final manifestation of His glory. Then and only then will all the wonderful promises and visions of material happiness and earthly peace for men be immediately fulfilled.

Objection and Answer

But, then, had Jesus a right to say even, "*Your sins are forgiven*"? The scribes who were "*sitting there, questioning in their hearts,*" said to themselves, "*Why does this man speak thus? It is blasphemy! Who can forgive sins but God alone?*"

It is obvious that the scribes were quite right in their assertion that God alone can forgive sins. The Old Testament teaches this clearly. The word in Isaiah, "I, I am He who blots out your transgression" (Is. XLIII. 5) means simply, "I and I alone forgive sins." We know ourselves that this is true. For a sinner to receive forgiveness means that God's heart has been miraculously opened in love towards him. But God alone can open His own heart in this way towards a sinner. For a sinner, receiving forgiveness means being given a pledge that in the day of judgment when the books are opened and the dead, great and small, stand before God, the record written against him will be blotted out and remembered no more, and his name will be found in the Lamb's book of life. But only God in His love can give any man such a pledge.

Moreover the Old Testament teaches that the cost of forgiveness is so great and terrible, that only God can pay it. Early in the history of Israel, Abraham was taught this lesson. He had been taught somehow in his own early days the crude lesson that only sacrifice could atone for sin. It was his custom when he wanted God's forgiveness to go to an altar and kill a ram and pour out its blood and burn it as a sacrifice to God. In this primitive way men were taught that what was wrong with life was so terrible and tragic that it could not be put right without some costly and painful solution. But one day God took him further and more deeply into the cost that must be paid for the forgiveness of sin. God said to Abraham "Take your son, your only son Isaac, whom you love, and go to the land of Moriah, and offer him there as a burnt offering upon one of the mountains of which I shall tell you" (Gen. xxii. 2). It was as if God was telling him that a greater sacrifice must be provided, a greater agony must be born if the cost of forgiveness was to be met, and God made Abraham undergo the agony of the long journey towards the mountain, of the dismal and terrible preparation for the slaughter of his only son. God allowed him to lift the knife for the final blow—and only then did God stop his hand and make him look up to see the lamb that He Himself had provided. Was not God saying, "No Abraham, not your lamb, not even your costliest lamb, will do to pay the price of sin. It must be *my* lamb, *my* agony, *my* sacrifice." Who can forgive sins but God alone, who gives for it His only Son "that whoever believes in Him should not perish but have eternal life" (Jn. iii. 16)?

But can even God forgive? When the children of Israel in the wilderness sinned, making and worshipping the golden calf and crying out for a return to Egypt, Moses had to plead with God for their forgiveness. And in his very prayer for such a mercy he expressed his deep feeling of doubt as to whether it was possible at all. "Alas," he cried, "this people have sinned a great sin; they have made for themselves gods of gold. But now, if thou wilt forgive their sin—and if not, blot me, I pray thee, out of thy book which thou hast written" (Ex. xxxii. 31–2). Is real forgiveness not the one thing that is "too hard for the Lord"? To us human beings it at times seems impossible that God should be able to cancel the eternal effects of our guilty and foolish past; for that past can show itself to be the most real and unalterable and inevitably crushing thing, barring all our hope of happiness.

Within our ordinary human relationships we are often forced to wonder if such a thing as forgiveness is ever possible. We can sometimes cure bodies, but can we ever cure wounded love? Can we restore a dear and beautiful human relationship that has become distorted or destroyed through sin and unfaithfulness? We can condone sin in another person, and try artificially to ignore and forget it. But is it possible for there ever to be between two human beings a forgiveness that can mean a creative and new start together as if the past had never happened?

No wonder, then, that the scribes, with thoughts like these in their minds, felt angry at Jesus for seeming to take forgiveness lightly when He pronounced the paralytic man absolved from his sins. But Jesus read their thoughts and admitted that their objection was a serious one in the very answer that He gave: "*Which is easier, to say to the paralytic, 'Your sins are forgiven,' or to say, 'Rise, take up your pallet and walk'?*" His reply is an assurance that He understands their objection and knows that it is no light thing even to speak of the possibility that sin can be forgiven. Indeed He asserts that it would be far easier to set about curing this man of his paralysis than to set about trying to solve the problem of his sin. To say, "Your sins are forgiven" is the most costly and agonising word the Son of man can utter.

Jesus is here thinking of, and facing up to, the meaning and purpose of His coming passion and death. As that time approached nearer to Him, He gathered His disciples together for the Passover feast in an upper room. "Now as they were eating, Jesus took bread, and blessed and broke it, and gave it to the disciples and said, 'Take, eat; this is my body.' And He took a cup, and when He had given thanks He gave it to them, saying, 'Drink of it, all of you; for this is the blood of the covenant, which is poured out for many for the forgiveness of sins' " (Mt. xxvi. 26–8). This is the why and wherefore of His approaching bitter passion and death. It is this passion and death that alone give Him the power on earth to forgive sins. His broken body and shed blood are the full and sufficient answer to the objection of the Scribes that He was treating the forgiveness of sins lightly. They proclaim not only that He knows the cost of God's being able to utter the word of forgiveness, but that He Himself has come to pay that cost in full, as only He could do. *"Which is easier, to say to the paralytic, 'Your sins are forgiven,' or to say, 'Rise, take up your pallet and walk' ?"*

SEAL AND SIGN

Jesus had, from the very moment He spoke His first word, forgiven this paralytic man his sins. Even if nothing else had happened in that house but the spoken word of forgiveness it would have been enough.

There the man lay at the feet of Jesus. Though he was still held down in physical impotence by his disease, the most wonderful miracle that God can accomplish for any man had happened to him. When Jesus Himself spoke the word of absolution there and then, without any sign of it being given, the greatest and most costly of all God's mighty and loving acts towards man had taken place—a soul was cleansed and renewed. Everything else that happened to this man that day was secondary, and simply illustrated and complemented what this first great miracle of forgiveness had accomplished.

But Jesus was not content to stop at that. He had answered in words the doubts of the scribes about His power to forgive sins. His final answer was a positive concrete proof that nothing could gainsay. " *'But that you may know that the Son of man has authority on earth to forgive sins'—he said to the paralytic—'I say to you, rise, take up your pallet and go home.' And he rose, and immediately took up the pallet and went out before them all.*" The outward miracle was the sign that the inward miracle had indeed taken place.

The crowd marvelled. *"They were all amazed and glorified God, saying, 'We never saw anything like this'."*

What Jesus wanted them to marvel at was not only the fact that a paralysed man had been made to walk, but the fact that, because he walked, his sins were really forgiven, that the Son of man indeed had *authority on earth to forgive sins*. As surely as His Word was powerful to release men from physical weakness so surely was it also powerful to release men from the guilt of sin. They had already seen His Word accomplishing great things in the realm of devil-possession and foul disease. Now they saw that His Word was powerful to work miracles where the problem is the guilty past, the fearful conscience, the stained soul, the eternal question mark hovering over man's final destiny, the wrath of God, the danger of judgment and Hell.

We must see all Jesus's miracles in this light. They are the signs that the Kingdom of God has broken into this world in such a hidden, yet real, way that men can now enjoy God's forgiveness and live their lives on a new basis of trust and love towards their heavenly Father. In this way they can indeed enter the Kingdom now and share its new life through faith in Jesus.

Miracles can still happen as signs that the Kingdom has come in this hidden way. Men can still experience in the realm of healing spectacular answers to prayer when they turn in faith to Christ. And time and again miraculous signs take place in the moral realm. Men's lives are changed, drunkards become sober, thieves become honest, men with foul tempers are made mild, the hopeless and despairing are enabled to rise and walk in newness of life, all as a consequence and sign that they have entered a new relationship of peace with God, and have been in contact with the transforming power of the Kingdom of God in our midst.

But miracles are always merely occasional and sporadic events, and Jesus did not wish to leave us to look only for miracles as signs of the presence of His Kingdom in our midst. The bread and wine of the Lord's Supper, the water of the Baptismal font are the concrete and permanent signs He has left with His Church that forgiveness of sins is real. His giving of the bread and wine, His washing of our bodies with water are meant to be to us the outward manifestation of His Kingdom in our midst, and of the way He Himself in the resurrection power of His Kingdom is indeed feeding us, cleansing us, uniting our lives to His glorious life. And all this is a pledge that one day the Kingdom of God which has already broken into the life of this world in such a wonderful yet hidden way, will break further into this world in all its manifest power and glory, and all the disease and pain and weakness and compromise that we at present have to bear even though we live under the sign of the Kingdom, will be banished for ever.

THE MAN WITH THE WITHERED
HAND

Again he entered the synagogue, and a man was there who had a withered hand. And they watched him, to see whether he would heal him on the sabbath, so that they might accuse him. And he said to the man who had the withered hand, "Come here." And he said to them, "Is it lawful on the sabbath to do good or to do harm, to save life or to kill?" But they were silent. And he looked around at them with anger, grieved at their hardness of heart, and said to the man, "Stretch out your hand." He stretched it out, and his hand was restored. The Pharisees went out, and immediately held counsel with the Herodians against him, how to destroy him.

Mk. III. 1–6.

The Grace of God in the Place of Worship on the Sabbath

"Again he entered the synagogue." Jesus was faithful in His attendance at the Jewish synagogue on the Sabbath. He had been brought up to observe the custom strictly as a habit of His life. The crowds of sight-seers at Deeside know that if they want to see members of the Royal Family they need only line up on the route from Balmoral to Crathie Church. Those in Galilee who wanted to be certain of meeting Jesus, knew that all they needed to do was to go on the Sabbath to the synagogue nearest where He was staying. There He was sure to be found.

It was fitting that Jesus should be found there. The synagogue had a special significance in Jewish life because it was the place where the Scriptures were read and expounded in public. God's people gathered there to hear and learn what God had to say to them through their Bible. But these Scriptures all pointed to Him, and His coming to be the Christ and Saviour. Surely the most likely place for Jesus to go to let men know who He is and to declare His presence among men was the synagogue on the Sabbath day where the Scriptures were opened to declare to God's people that their Messiah would one day come to redeem them and all mankind.

33

If we want to find Jesus today, the most likely place is still the place where on the day of His resurrection, the Scriptures that witness to Him are read and expounded. "Jesus Christ is the same yesterday and today and for ever" (Heb. XIII. 9). We know that Jesus is to be found today doing many of the wonderful things we see Him doing in the Gospels. He is to be found healing the sick, confronting men and calling them to leave all and follow Him, forgiving the penitent sinners and receiving their adoration. He is also to be found regularly visiting the place where His people gather each week to read and to seek to understand the Word of the Lord. Of course we must not imagine that He is to be found only in this place on the Christian Sabbath day. How can we confine to one holy place and to one holy day the grace of Jesus Christ who moved about continually through all the towns and cities of Galilee every day and who ate and drank with publicans and sinners? But it is even more true today than it was in Galilee nineteen hundred years ago, that if we want to be sure of meeting Jesus Christ, we need not go here and there vaguely in the hope that we will come across Him somehow. Rather we need only go on our Sabbath day to the place where the people of God meet around the Holy Scriptures to worship God. It is a tragedy that so many people miss Him because they will not observe this simple fact.

Jesus went to the synagogue that Sabbath day in spite of the fact that He knew that most of them either did not want Him or did not believe in Him. A week or two earlier, the authorities of this synagogue at Capernaum had behaved very unpleasantly to Him and had shown Him a good deal of virulent antagonism. But here He was, back again. We, ourselves, can thank God that Jesus is so patient. When we think of what we are and how we behave within the Church today, when we think also of how our authorities and Church courts sometimes behave towards Jesus Christ, how difficult it is to convince ourselves sometimes that He will take the trouble to come back into our midst so regularly on the Sabbath day! But the grace of God in Jesus Christ is too faithful and powerful to be put off easily by the folly and indifference and enmity with which we sometimes treat Him. Do not let us despair of His coming here in His grace to be in our midst.

THE GRACE OF GOD CONFRONTED BY THE CHALLENGE OF MAN'S ECONOMIC NEED

"And a man was there who had a withered hand." When Jesus viewed the congregation in this synagogue what first met His eye and claimed His attention was a man about whom the first thing to strike an onlooker would be, not his great piety, but his sheer material poverty. He had a withered hand, and Jesus said, *"Come here."*

Let us look at this man as Jesus looked at him. His withered hand stands for his unemployment. He is unable to do a day's work. Tradition says that this man was a stonemason by trade. He had lost the power of his arm. There was no unemployment benefit in those days and no compulsory employment of disabled persons. This man represents many in the world today who are oppressed by the threat of poverty, worried about work and home. He is the frail member of a ruthless society where only the strong tend to survive. This was the man to whom Jesus from the start gave special attention in the synagogue on that Sabbath day. This was the aspect of human need that He directly addressed Himself to. He singled him out with a very direct message, "Look, I see what is worrying you, and I can and will do something about it. I can speak a word that will mean money for you, a job for you, a better and more comfortable home." Here we have the grace of God in the synagogue, taking up in a very direct way the challenge of man's economic needs.

Now the man was completely surprised. He had never related in his mind what went on in this synagogue with the needs of his everyday life or the injustices and problems he had to put up with in this world. He had not gone expecting any such word from Jesus, and he had not in any way pushed himself or his need in front of Jesus. To him the synagogue was not the place where one could expect to find the problems of life met and solved like this. And the synagogue authorities were themselves utterly shocked that a miracle that should have been done on Monday was done on Sunday.

Many people are like them in their thinking. They divorce Sunday worship from their real present life-situation. Their idea of what should happen in Church on Sunday is something on a

level that never directly touches or affects the economic needs
and pressing social and political problems that cause men real
anxiety and face them with a ruthless struggle from Monday to
Saturday. The ideal worship, they think, is something designed
to enable them to forget these mundane tensions and struggles
for a while, in an exercise of soul that lifts them up above all
this, inspiring them if only for a moment with fine feelings of
exultation. After such a divine exercise they will feel better
able to face the unaltered and unalterable world of everyday
life. The word they expect to hear in the Church is a word
constantly exhorting them to piety, a word that speaks a great
deal about sin and forgiveness, inward experiences and states
of soul, God and Heaven and Hell. But, they imagine, the problems of this hard life, politics and employment prospects, working conditions and the distribution of money, are problems on a
level with which the Word of God in the Church has no direct
concern.

Now of course we are right to realise and to assert that there
is a realm beyond and above the realm of the material and
political pressures and needs that make life so full of problems
and tensions for most men today. There is the Kingdom of God
above and beyond, into which a man must enter to be saved.
We must preach this Kingdom. And we are right to stress the
importance of the realities that lie behind such words as sin and
forgiveness, Heaven and Hell, God and faith and salvation. We
must speak often and clearly about such themes because the
Bible speaks often and clearly about such things. If a man tries
to live without facing the problems raised by such realities he
is a fool indeed.

But we must not try to divorce this Kingdom of God from the
harsh world of economic need, with its intense problems and
pressures, into which men have to go when they leave our
Sunday worship. Jesus in the synagogue that Sabbath brought
the grace of God directly to bear on the economic needs of the
man He addressed. He had for him a word, the bearing of
which on his everyday life was perfectly clear. The Kingdom of
God, of which we speak to men in His name, is not merely a
realm of blessedness above and beyond. It is also a Kingdom in
our midst that grows and spreads in our midst through the
Word that proclaims it, and it affects the whole material and

political and economic realm of man's life radically by the pressure of its hidden spread and growth. This means that those of us who preach on Sundays in the name of Christ as well as speaking about Heaven and Hell, and sin and forgiveness, and God and salvation, must also remember that many of those to whom we speak of such things often suffer from poverty and financial anxiety, from social injustices, from the devastation of war, from cruel and wasting diseases. Surely as we face such needy people in the name of Jesus Christ we will at times be given a word that will interfere immediately and directly and radically for their material well-being, in the social and political affairs of our country. Let us not be afraid of hearing at times a word from the pulpit that has direct political implications. And as for those of us, like this man with the withered hand, whose lives are filled with cares and problems that we perhaps try to dismiss from our minds and hearts in order on the Sabbath day "to be in the mood" for worship and for God's Word, let us learn that He understands our need better than we can understand it ourselves. He wants to have fellowship with us not simply by lifting up our souls into His heavenly realm, but by Himself coming down into the midst of our need with His divine power to make all things new.

The Grace of God encountered by the hardness of Men's hearts

In the very place where He was seeking to meet this case of dire human need, Jesus encountered the most sinister opposition. The Pharisees were there in the synagogue and they were ready to take whatever action they could to prevent Him from fulfilling His work of grace.

The Pharisees were behaving stupidly in their opposition to Jesus. Suppose that a great match is due to take place in a few months' time on a certain cricket field. The greenkeeper is told specially to prepare the pitch and guard it, keeping off all intruders. He does so zealously. He spends days and hours in preparation. He puts his heart and soul into the work. He almost identifies himself with this pitch that looks so beautiful and is perfect for playing on. But then he begins to be stupid. He forgets the coming match, and the great reason why he has had to prepare and keep this pitch. He begins to guard this pitch simply for the sake of the selfish satisfaction it gives him to see the beautiful effect of his skill and craftsmanship. And when the time for the match comes, he ruins his career as groundsman by a great and stubborn refusal to hand over and to let anyone spoil his pitch by using it for the game. So it was with the Pharisees. God had appointed them as the representatives of the Jewish nation to guard the truth of the Word of God, to guard the synagogue and the Sabbath day and the Temple. They were to see that these things were kept till the One who was the true Word of God and the Lord of the synagogue and the Sabbath and the Temple should come and take over from them, and teach them their true meaning. But now the Word of God, the Lord of the synagogue and the Sabbath and the Temple was in their midst. Now was the day when they should recognise Him and hand over their responsibility. But they had come to regard themselves as Lords over the synagogue, Sabbath and Temple. Instead of remembering that they were simply stewards and servants they said to Jesus, "This is our day, not yours. We are the lords here and you must conform to our rules and standards or we will exclude you and kill you," for on that very day they *went out, and immediately held counsel with the Herodians against him, how to destroy him."*

Jesus forced them there and then to realise what they were doing. He made the man whom He was going to heal stand in front of Him. *"Is it lawful,"* He said, *"on the sabbath to do good or to do harm, to save life or to kill?"* What were they really doing in seeking to prevent Him from doing His merciful work in this place of worship? They were harming this man He was trying to heal. They were murderers for they were really killing where He had come to seek to give salvation and life. This was the accusation He hurled at them, and as He did so they could see in His face that they were being warned in dead earnest of a crime that was terrible. *"He looked around at them with anger, grieved at their hardness of heart."* He was filled with anger because by their attitude they were preventing the grace of God from meeting human need.

Let us always remember His words. We too are the guardians of the Church, His Church, in our generation. Some of us sit on its courts, decide about the use of its buildings, about whether or not there is to be a real attempt to bring other people in—

and what kind of people we want in. All of us by our attitude decide what kind of a welcome people are going to have in our midst when they come in with their need. Let us remember that the greatest sin that the keepers of the Church can commit is to do anything to prevent the grace of God from meeting human need within the House of God—either by indifference or stupidity, or antagonism. For the Pharisees to seek to do this was in the sight of our Lord "*to kill.*" For us to do the same in our day is no less murderous.

The Grace of God responded to by Human Decision and Faith

The man with the withered hand had himself to make a decision. Whom did he believe? Which side was he going to take in this conflict? Standing before him was Jesus, offering to save his life, and proclaiming that the Law and the Sabbath were sacred only as God used them for the purposes of such salvation. He was being summoned to respond to the living Word of God in Jesus. But he had been taught, from a child, a tradition about the Law and the Sabbath that was sacred and inviolable and more important than even God's mercy. Watching him closely were the Pharisees, his teachers. He must choose either to obey the living Word of God, or conform to their deadly tradition. His decision to respond to the Living Word of God needed courage, for the Pharisees were his rulers and their hearts were bent on murder.

The living Word, or dead and deadening tradition? This is still an issue in the Church of today. What sacred things is Christ asking us to put second to the demands of the living Word He has to speak to us today? Perhaps it is not our Pharisaism or our Sabbatarianism at all, but our Presbyterianism or our Episcopalianism which may be hindering His saving work, and the advance of the Church into a new fullness. Or it may be some form of ritual that suited our forefathers but which no longer allows the grace of God to reach the needs of men in the twentieth century. We must be careful not to "make the Word of God void by our tradition" (Mk. vii. 13).

The living Word that Jesus spoke was powerful enough to enable His hearer to do what was commanded. "*Stretch out your hand,*" said Jesus to him. It was impossible. His hand was withered and his arm was impotent. But he did it. The Word of Jesus was strong enough to overcome his own impotence.

When men hear the Word of God, new possibilities are born within them through the powerful Word that they hear. This is so because the Word of God creates faith, and faith can remove mountains. It was by faith that this man stretched out his hand, and in doing so his faith rose to the new possibilities that were offered to him in the Word that Jesus spoke. Let us listen to what He is commanding us to do, throwing away our fears that we might not be able to do it. He does not mock us in what He commands us. His command implies that we can fulfil it, certainly not through our own powers, but through the power that His very command brings to us. My word "shall not return to me empty, but it shall accomplish that which I purpose, and prosper in the thing for which I sent it" (Is. LV. 11).

THE HEALING OF THE
CENTURION'S SLAVE

After he had ended all his sayings in the hearing of the people he entered Capernaum. Now a centurion had a slave who was dear to him, who was sick and at the point of death. When he heard of Jesus, he sent to him elders of the Jews, asking him to come and heal his slave. And when they came to Jesus, they besought him earnestly, saying, "He is worthy to have you do this for him, for he loves our nation, and he built us our synagogue." And Jesus went with them. When he was not far from the house, the centurion sent friends to him, saying to him, "Lord, do not trouble yourself, for I am not worthy to have you come under my roof; therefore I did not presume to come to you. But say the word, and let my servant be healed. For I am a man set under authority, with soldiers under me: and I say to one, 'Go,' and he goes; and to another, 'Come,' and he comes; and to my slave, 'Do this,' and he does it." When Jesus heard this he marveled at him, and turned and said to the multitude that followed him, "I tell you, not even in Israel have I found such faith." And when those who had been sent returned to the house, they found the slave well.

Lk. vii. 1–10.

Jesus marvelled at the faith of this Roman Centurion. It seemed so wonderful to Him that He drew the attention of His disciples to it, and its appearance in one who was a Gentile filled His heart with hope for the whole world. Matthew reports Jesus as exclaiming, after listening to the man, "Truly I say to you, not even in Israel have I found such faith, I tell you many will come from east and west and sit at table with Abraham, Isaac and Jacob in the Kingdom of Heaven" (Mt. viii. 10–11).

Whatever made Jesus "marvel" must be regarded as something of supreme importance. We are not told that He marvelled when He saw His own miracles of healing taking place before His eyes. He uttered no expression of wonder when at His word in the storm the wind ceased and there was a great calm. We do not find Him marvelling at the finest human works of skill and art, for when the disciples pointed to the temple saying, "Look, Teacher, what wonderful stones and what wonderful

41

buildings," He simply replied, "Do you see these great build-ings? There will not be left here one stone upon the other, that will not be thrown down" (Mk. XIII. 2). But here we find Him filled with admiration, and calling on His disciples to share it with Him, at the evidence of great faith within a human mind and heart.

We must remember, too, that this Roman Centurion had many other sterling qualities which we might expect Jesus to appraise highly. In an age in Roman society when slaves were normally regarded as having little right to any human con-sideration, this man showed for his own slave a deep and anxious concern. He showed a great deal of genuine humility in his approach to Jesus—also a rare virtue in a Roman colonial in those days. He was a generous benefactor of religion. He had built a local synagogue, and his character and disposition were such that he had plenty of friends flocking round him in his need, ready to go on his errands and commend him to Jesus. He had all these other virtues, yet Jesus singled out no virtue for His commendation except his faith, at which He marvelled and said that He had not found the like anywhere in Israel.

"HE LOVES OUR NATION AND HE BUILT FOR US OUR SYNAGOGUE"

The first sign of his faith was that he loved the people to whom God had especially given the gift of faith and the book of faith. He was without doubt a well-educated man of the world brought up under the influence of the Roman and Greek culture of his time. He knew the worth of what was best in the religion and philosophy of that ancient world. He knew what Athens and Rome had to give him. But when he came to choose on what he was going ultimately to rest and support his mind and soul, he chose not the highest and best that the culture of Greece and Rome could offer him, but the religion of the Jews. He found that the hunger of his soul was satisfied not by the great ideas of men like Plato and Socrates but by the Word of the God of Israel. Not the god of the wise men of this world but the God of Abraham, Isaac and Jacob became his God. The Jewish Bible became to him the book in which he found the true light of life. In these Hebrew Scriptures he found satisfaction and truth, and a sure Word that gave his life stability and hope. In the faith of this people in their Lord and His Word, he found at last the key, and the only key, to the meaning of life and to the way that life should be lived. He found all this in the fellowship of the Jewish people in the synagogue at Capernaum where he was taught the meaning of these Scriptures. There his faith became so strong that he obviously began to understand the truth better than his teachers. All this meant so much to him that he showed his gratitude by a great act of munificence. *"He loves our nation and he built for us our synagogue."*

It is a sure sign of true faith that it instinctively turns to the Holy Scriptures to find the Word on which it must rest and the truth on which it must feed itself. The man who has faith, even though he may know everything else that the world can teach him in the realm of culture and science and philosophy, will nevertheless turn instinctively to the Bible for the light he still needs in order to understand the meaning of life and death, the meaning of history, and the meaning of such words as God, and evil, and sin. Certainly he will enjoy all the other great books in the world beside the Bible, but in the Word which comes from the heart of the Bible alone, he will find Jesus Christ and the light and life and sustaining power by which his faith began, and through which his faith must always continue to live. The man of faith is inevitably a man of the Bible. The man who says he has faith, and yet can leave the Bible neglected and unheeded is deceived in saying that he has faith.

Faith, today, is bound to inspire not only a love for the Bible, but also a concern for the destiny and salvation of Israel, the people of God. Jesus's word to the woman at the well of Samaria, "Salvation is from the Jews" (Jn. IV. 22), is a continual reminder to the Church that Christianity is the true development and fulfilment of the faith that is the heritage and birthright of this uniquely called nation that has so often been despised and abused by the Christian world.

"I AM NOT WORTHY TO HAVE YOU COME UNDER MY ROOF"

What this centurion felt and saw in the presence of Jesus is another sign of his faith. He wanted Jesus to come. He sent for

Him. But then, as he waited, the thought of this man's coming into his humble dwelling began to overwhelm him. How would he receive Him? What would he offer Him? He must not have Him too near. One account of the incident says he sent some of his friends (another story says he went himself), to beg Jesus not to come nearer but to speak the Word that would bring life to his dear slave.

This is remarkable. Other people did not mind being near Jesus. They opened their doors to Him with readiness. Simon the Pharisee felt no qualms about asking Him to supper and then both neglecting and patronising Him when He arrived at his house. Many of His contemporaries did not mind in the least how familiarly they treated Him.

In the presence of Jesus, this man felt and saw something that most other men did not feel or see at all. He gave a hint of what he felt and saw, when he sent the message, *"Lord, do not trouble yourself, for I am not worthy to have you come under my roof; therefore I did not presume to come to you. But say the word, and let my servant be healed. For I am a man set under authority, with soldiers under me: and I say to one, 'Go,' and he goes; and to another, 'Come,' and he comes; and to my slave, 'Do this,' and he does it."* He saw in Jesus One who, he believed, merely needed to speak and His will would be accomplished. His thought was going back to the Old Testament scriptures which he now knew so well. There it is taught that God need only speak a Word, and His will is effected. In the beginning God said, "Let there be," and there was (Gen. i. 3). "For He spoke, and it came to be; He commanded, and it stood forth" (Ps. xxxiii. 9). The centurion saw and felt that God, with all His living creative power, was somehow there present in Jesus. Jesus had but to utter His voice and his slave would be healed. This Roman had the power to see behind the lowly outward form of the carpenter of Nazareth nothing less than the presence among men of the divine creative Word that was there in the beginning of all things. He saw in Jesus the same glory as Peter saw when he fell at His feet in the boat crying, "Depart from me, for I am a sinful man, O Lord" (Lk. v. 8), and when, later on, his eyes were opened even more and he confessed Him, "You are the Christ, the Son of the living God" (Mt. xvi. 16). It was because the Centurion saw this in Jesus that he was appalled by the thought that the

Lord should come near him or enter his house. But those of His time who could so easily rub shoulders with Him, compliment Him or insult Him according to their moods, saw nothing at all, where this man saw so much.

Faith, then, sees and feels and knows in the presence of Jesus that this man, human as He is, nevertheless possesses as His own right whatever belongs to God alone. Indeed, the power to see what is utterly unique and holy in the person and presence of Jesus is the power of faith. Faith is the gift of new eyes to see the glory of God in the face of Jesus Christ, the Lord, to penetrate behind the outward personality of this humble man and recognise that here in His presence is none other than the living God, mighty to judge and to save.

What this centurion saw and felt in the presence of Jesus, then, marked him out as a man of great faith. Faith still gives to those who have it the characteristic of being able to see, in the midst of a world where many do not see. Today many can look at Jesus Christ as He is presented in the New Testament and they can see in Him no more than a divine teacher, others can confess Him still as Lord and God. It is faith that makes the difference. Some can see in the Church of Christ no more significance than would belong to any group of people interested in being religious together. But others can look at the same Church and see it indeed as the body of Christ permeated by the hidden glory of God and vital with the life of the Kingdom of God, the meeting place of heaven and earth. It is faith that makes the difference in what men see. Some can see in the Sacraments of Baptism and the Lord's Supper simply interesting and eloquent ceremonies, useful religious rites to be carefully observed in obedience to the command of Jesus. Others see the same Sacraments as the means by which the living Christ gives Himself to His Church, inserts His living members into His body, and feeds and preserves His people with heavenly sustenance. Again it is faith that enables them to see that to which others are blind. Some look on preaching simply as the word of a man who may be so good and wise and well worth listening to that no better word of man could be heard anywhere. But others find in the preaching of Holy Scripture nothing less than the Word of the living God, and it is faith that enables them to see this.

"But say the Word, and let my Servant be healed"

The centurion asked simply for a word from Jesus. That would be enough. He did not ask proof that the word Jesus spoke concerning his servant would be fulfilled. If Jesus spoke the word assuring him that all was well, all was bound to be well, no matter what he saw before his eyes. What concerned him was to hear the word rather than to see the proof. The word was sufficient for his faith. This is another remarkable feature of faith. It is content to cling to the Word of God. It finds such reality and power and assurance in hearing the Word of God that it can face, if need be, disappointment and delay and long weary years of waiting in serene trust that the Word that it has heard will indeed be fulfilled, and that it will one day see that fulfilment. If sight and experience is delayed, faith can live by the Word alone.

We have to learn in the life of faith to be content with the Word. Often in life God asks us to trust His Word alone on a matter, assures us that His Word is true, and refuses us proof or signs that this is so. And He expects us to find His mere Word sufficient. God sends us out to work for Him. He promises that no work that is done in His name will be in vain. "In the Lord your labour is not in vain," His Word says to us (1 Cor. xv. 58). Yet we sometimes see no proof of this. Indeed we sometimes have to labour and see our labour apparently go in vain. God expects us in this matter to trust His Word alone, without signs, without proof. He gives us through His Word the assurance that we are righteous and perfect in His sight in Jesus Christ our Lord. In His Word He addresses us as His children. He numbers us amongst the people whom Christ has saved, who have died and risen in Him, who are clothed for ever in His perfect righteousness and holiness. This is how His Word speaks to us. But when we look at ourselves we do not see this. Indeed what we see tells us the opposite and contradicts the Word we have heard. For we see no sign in our hearts that we are saved and already made perfect in holiness in Christ. We see sin and failure and misery and despair within us. Yet God's Word continues to contradict everything we see. God expects us to believe in the Word and to live by the Word and to act as if the Word were more true than our own experience. And this is what faith can do. It asks for the Word and finds contentment with the Word alone. It can steady itself on the Word and wait long for its sure fulfilment.

"LORD, DO NOT TROUBLE YOURSELF"

The contentment of faith with the Word means that faith tends to abhor any fuss. This centurion in pleading with Jesus to speak only a word said to Him, "*Lord, do not trouble yourself.*" If he had the Word there was no need for Jesus to go all the way to the bedside of the sick lad to lay His hands upon him, or to breathe life into him. If the Lord would speak the Word, all further ceremony or procession could be avoided. "*Lord, do not trouble yourself.*" Where there is faith there is always this tendency to lay such exclusive stress on the Word that further ceremony becomes of little significance. Where faith is weak signs and ceremonies become necessary. In many of His cases, Jesus, besides speaking His healing Word, took the trouble of going all the way to meet them, to lay His hands on them. Indeed on some occasions He used spittle and clay to convince their weak faith that He was seeking to help them. But He always sought to make people realise that it was by the Word He mainly sought to heal them and not primarily by such ceremonies. Faith recognises this and is willing often to be content with the Word without troubling the Lord any further.

Jesus has troubled Himself to give us more than His Word within the Church today. He has given us His Word as our main source of comfort and life, but He has also given us two simple sacraments, Baptism and the Lord's Supper to help our weak faith which so often needs and asks for more than the Word. In and through the sacraments Jesus confirms and completes what He seeks to do through the Word, and this is why the sacraments are called seals of the Word. Our faith needs the sacraments. It will use them and reverence them as precious signs and means given to us by Jesus Christ Himself to help our faith and to keep us near Himself. How can we ever neglect the signs He seeks to give us? But if our faith is real it will always rest in the Word. It will use the sacraments as means by which it is brought back again and again to the true meaning and power of the Word. And it will abhor any attempt to invent further elaborate ceremonies that can only obscure the simplic ity and power of the Word that the living Christ is able to speak in order to save and strengthen His people today. It is a weak and distorted and debased faith that demands the evolution of elaborate and troublesome ritual, because it cannot find satisfaction in the Word. A real and living faith when it hears the Word of God will always tend to say, "Lord, do not trouble yourself any further."

THE RAISING OF THE WIDOW'S SON

Soon afterward he went to a city called Nain, and his disciples and a great crowd went with him. As he drew near to the gate of the city, behold, a man who had died was being carried out, the only son of his mother, and she was a widow; and a large crowd from the city was with her. And when the Lord saw her, he had compassion on her and said to her, "Do not weep." And he came and touched the bier, and the bearers stood still. And he said, "Young man, I say to you, arise." And the dead man sat up, and began to speak. And he gave him to his mother. Fear seized them all; and they glorified God, saying, "A great prophet has arisen among us!" and "God has visited his people!" And this report concerning him spread through the whole of Judea and all the surrounding country.

Lk. VII. 11–17.

INVITATION TO NAIN

It is remarkable that Jesus should have gone to visit Nain at this period of His ministry. He was then at the height of His popularity amongst the crowds in the towns of Galilee. Every moment of His time could have been fully absorbed in a very influential and fruitful ministry there at the centre of things. People were responsive and were taking in His message. Why should He leave these eager crowds and go to Nain? It was only a little village in a very remote part of the countryside, miles off the beaten track. A journey there meant a day or two's absence from many who needed Him at a critical time in His career.

Certainly Nain had once been a famous place in the religious traditions of the people of Israel. In the old days it had been called Shunem. It was one of the women of Shunem who had helped the prophet Elisha in his ministry and to whom God, as a reward, had given a son by a great miracle. This son, later on, died. Thereupon his mother made a famous journey in search of Elisha and compelled him to go back to Nain with her to raise the child from the dead.

We can only conjecture that He was invited to go there. Some of the people of Nain had seen Him doing miracles and had heard Him preaching perhaps at Capernaum or at some other country town in the area. As they watched Him, a vision of what He could do in their own little township filled their minds. They had been deeply concerned about the state of affairs in their little community. The people were forgetting God and neglecting their religious heritage. But they remembered how in the great old days of Shunem, Elisha had been compelled by a mother's faith and persistent pleading to come back to their village and work his miracle. Why should they not follow her example, and try to compel this new prophet Jesus who had arisen, to come back their way and do some wonderful new things in their day for the life of their village? Perhaps He would be able to show the people that the God, who had once done such great things, was not yet dead, but still living and powerful and that they need not think of Him only as One who once was almighty. Perhaps through Jesus, God would once again visit His people in Nain.

They spoke in this way to Jesus when they pleaded with Him to come. It no doubt took a good deal of faith and courage for them to invite Him. How thrilled they were when He decided and started out, under their leadership, on the way.

Is Nain not typical of the rural areas of our land today? We tend to deceive ourselves about the state of religion in our country districts. When we catch a first glimpse of a beautiful little country church commanding a magnificent sight of the natural glory of the earth in a churchyard marked by the tombs of covenanting martyrs, we are apt to become sentimental. We imagine that here at least it will be easy to find true worship and living religious zeal! But when we look closely at the situation, we find that in actual fact our country areas present as great a challenge to the Church as the "down town" parts of our cities with fewer hopeful features. Most of our cities and towns at the heart of them have strong movements of religious activity and life, and those who live there have frequent opportunities of finding out in various ways that men are putting Christ to the test, and proving His power to do marvellous things for men and women and life-situations in the twentieth century. But easy transport and modern means of mass-communication seem able to bring every kind of influence into rural life except the living influence and power of the Gospel.

But the visit of Jesus to Nain reminds us that there is hope for the rural areas today as well as for our cities. Nain reminds us that Jesus Christ is concerned to visit the out-of-the-way places as well as large centres of population. It reminds us, also, however, that He may still be waiting for an invitation to Him to come. It is remarkable how readily He responded to invitations from men and women to visit their homes, their weddings, their villages—even at times when He seemed to be wholly absorbed in more important matters. It is remarkable too that one of the stories of the resurrection appearances of Jesus tells of how two disciples "constrained him" (Lk. xxiv. 29) with a pressing invitation that seemed to change His mind, to enter their home and sup with them. Since Jesus Christ showed Himself so willing to be diverted from the centre of things, let us have hope for our out-of-the-way places and situations and congregations.

A Gesture of Majesty and Compassion

Those who brought Jesus with them to Nain could not have staged anything more dramatic as His introduction to their village than the incident which took place at the gate on His arrival.

Jesus had brought a great crowd of people along with Him on His journey up the hillside. Those who surrounded Him were joyful and light-hearted. Many of them were now His disciples. They rejoiced because they now had hope for mankind. Jesus had already given clear signs in the miracles He had done that liberty and peace could come to men held down under the bondage of evil and corruption and decay. In their eyes Jesus was the bearer of new life and health for mankind. There was an excited stir in their midst as they toiled together up the final stages of the little hill road—the one road of access which travellers tell us is still used today. Was it not this road that the great prophet Elisha had used when he came to do his wonderful works in their midst centuries before?

But on their arrival at the gate of the village they discovered that a tragedy indeed had happened. A huge funeral procession, complete with hired mourners and a doleful band of musicians with cymbals and flutes, was coming to meet them, filing its way through the gate from the desolate main street, and making for the burial ground. At a glance Jesus and those who followed Him would be able to tell the nature of the tragedy that had stricken the little town. They could see the funeral bier with the body either wrapped in cloths or in a simple wicker coffin, carried slowly on by the bearers, and the chief mourner was a solitary woman. She was a widow and had lost her only son, her last human comfort and support.

The contrast between these two converging crowds was described by one of the fathers of the Church as "life meeting death." Here we have Jesus brought publicly face to face with the great ultimate problem that darkens, embitters and destroys so much of our human life that men question the love and power of God, and the sanity of existence. If He has no answer to this problem is it worth while listening to His answer to any other human problem? If He now stands helpless before the public and His own disciples in face of this inescapable situation can He indeed continue to claim that He has come to give men life and to give it more abundantly? It is indeed a dramatic and tense encounter, and there are many witnesses. If Jesus could not raise this dead child here and now, He could not be the saviour of men.

In this situation He made one of His most majestic gestures. "*Do not weep,*" He said to the mother. "*And he came and touched the bier, and the bearers stood still.*" Perhaps nowhere else did Jesus reveal in His bearing such imperious and calm authority. He deliberately and quietly stopped the funeral procession. The bearers and all their followers found themselves suddenly arrested by One who seemed to claim for Himself the right to take command in even the most tragic of human situations. Jesus acted as if He were One who had come finally and decisively to interfere with the doleful and dismal procession of human life towards destruction and the graveyard. It was as if He were publicly saying "Hitherto I have proved my power supreme in the realm where men lie bound by insanity and disease and infirmity. Now I claim for myself the realm of death!" In laying His hand upon the coffin it is as if Jesus was acting like a king with great plans of conquest who with his generals looks over a map spread before him, lays his hand on territory hitherto unoccupied by his forces and says, "This also must now come under my dominion."

In this sudden dramatic gesture of Jesus, we must see a sign not only of His authority and power, but also of His human compassion. The mood of the whole crowd supporting the bereaved woman was one of sympathetic pity, and Jesus, along with everyone else there, gave that too. The dead boy was "*the only son of his mother, and a large crowd from the city was with her. And when the Lord saw her, he had compassion on her and said to her, 'Do not weep.' And he came and touched the bier.*" Jesus was so human that He shared the feelings and perfectly expressed the sentiments of the crowd. He has become one with the crowd of us in those strange feelings of humanity for suffering humanity without the expression of which man becomes indeed worse than a beast. Perhaps He would also have been moved as ordinary human nature is moved by the excitement of a football match or a great national occasion. The New Testament as it tells us about Him, often underlines this simple fact of the compassionate humanity of Jesus. To feel with the crowd as He did, is natural and human, and it was this ordinary humanity that Jesus Christ took upon Himself when He became man. He took it upon Himself in order to redeem it from the evil and perversion and distortion that find their expression in the mob brutality and hatefulness that are manifest at the Cross.

For us to be Christian, then, does not mean that we have to become unnatural. Certainly we must "deny ourselves" in a very radical way (Mt. xvi. 24). We must in many ways live differently from the majority of people in this present "world" with its fashions and demands (Rom. xii. 1). But this does not mean that we have to deny ourselves the normal expression of the impulses and instincts that make us "human," and that most people recognise as belonging to "humanity," and as making human beings better than the beasts. Indeed we must deliberately set such ordinary humanity before us as one of our aims in life. When the Apostle pleads with the early Christians at Colossae to "put on . . . compassion" (Col. iii. 12), he is simply appealing to them to seek to show the same humanity as Jesus did when in the midst of the crowd, moved by the feelings that He shared in common with them, He said "*Do not weep*" and put out his hand and touched the coffin that held her son.

A number of commentators see an even deeper significance in this gesture of Jesus in touching the dead body. When He came to earth and entered so fully into our human life, our Lord's purpose was to go to the Cross and there finally take upon Himself the whole burden and bitterness and consequences of our human sin. This had to be. He came to give us life and freedom, but in giving us such life He had to take upon Himself our death, bondage and guilt. This is why He came so close to us and made Himself so much one with us. If He intended to take our sin and death from us He had to come close to it. If He intended to give us His life, He had to come close to us. Sometimes He gave us signs of all this. His touching the leper, for instance, was a sign that He was going to identify Himself in the closest association with all the filth and contamination of our human nature in order to clean it away. His breathing His breath over the disciples after the Resurrection was a similar sign that now in the Spirit He was going to remain so close to them that they could now share His life and peace and righteousness. So in this incident of raising the widow's son He gives another sign of how closely He is going to identify Himself with us in death in order to be able to give us life. "By touching the coffin," says Calvin, "He intended perhaps to show that He would by no means shrink from death and the grave in order to obtain life for us. He not only deigns to touch us with His hand in order to quicken us when we are dead, but, in order that He might raise us to heaven, Himself descends to the grave."

The Word of Resurrection and Restoration

Jesus raised the dead by His Word. *"And he said, 'Young man, I say to you, arise!' And the dead man sat up, and began to speak."* We think of His own words, "Truly, truly, I say to you, the hour is coming, and now is, when the dead will hear the voice of the Son of God, and those who hear will live" (Jn. v. 25).

Many commentators are impressed by the ease with which Jesus speaks this Word and raises the dead. "As easily as we awaken a sleeper, Jesus raises the dead." They compare the ease with which Jesus did this, with the prayer and effort required by the prophets Elijah and Elisha before they could raise the dead (I Kings XVII. 19–22; II Kings IV. 32–4).

But we must not be deceived into thinking that to speak this Word and accomplish the greatest of miracles, cost Jesus no effort. Jesus raised the dead with such ease only because He Himself laid hold of death. The majesty with which He raised the dead is inseparable from the love and compassion which made Him identify Himself with those under the bondage and power of death. Indeed, He is Lord over death because He gave Himself to death. Ultimately it was only because He had gone through death that He was able to say to His disciples, "All authority in heaven and on earth has been given to me" (Mt. xxviii. 18).

Moreover, it is significant that in this incident He raised the dead not simply by a word, but by contact with His own body which He was going to devote to death and agony. Therefore if the Word of Christ has power to raise the dead, that is because along with the word He speaks, He always put forth the love and power and life that was in Himself, the manifestation of which we see in His own death of self-giving on the Cross. That is why when He wishes to communicate to us today this love and power and life, He not only gives us His Word afresh, but also the sacrament of His broken body and shed blood. As one of the great fathers of the church, Cyril, writes "He performs the miracle not only in word, but also touches the bier to the end that you might know that the sacred body of Christ is powerful to the saving of a man. For it is the body of life, and the flesh of the omnipotent Word whose power it possesses. For as iron applied to fire does the work of fire, so the flesh when it is united to the Word, which quickens all things, becomes itself also quickening and the banisher of death."

The Word of Christ brought not only resurrection from the dead, but the restoration of a broken human relationship. "*And the dead man sat up, and began to speak. And he gave him to his mother.*" This is what we know He can do through the forgiveness of sins and through His reconciling power in the midst of our homes today. In many a home there is a barrier even worse than death itself thwarting all expression of love and separating those whom God meant to be bound together. Hearts that once found true partnership and fellowship in one another are now frigid and frustrated, and lips that once could speak in freedom and love are now silent and unexpressive. Here where love was meant to reign, something worse than death now reigns over silence and grief. We can think of the relationship that, for years before his conversion, prevailed between Augustine and his mother Monica to whom it seemed that her son had become to her like someone alienated and dead in his indifference to God and coldness towards what she felt was alone worth living for.

Yet even this can be changed. As in this story the dead son *"sat up and began to speak,"* and Jesus *"delivered him to his mother,"* so today He can open hearts again in love to their dear ones, and make hitherto silent lips to speak in new tones that bring joy and hope where there has been despair and death. It was so when Augustine was converted by the Word of Christ. The miracle of inward resurrection that had taken place within him immediately manifested itself in an entirely new relationship between him and his mother. They began to be able to speak together. This is indeed the greatest of all the miracles that Christ has come to do for us—to restore even here and now the broken human relationship between husband and wife, parent and child, friend and friend, master and servant, class and class, race and race, so that there comes to be free and spontaneous communication and fellowship where there has been silence, sullenness and suspicion.

The restoration of such broken relationships is greater than any spectacular raising of dead bodies from their coffins or graves. It is the breaking and destruction of death in its worst aspect and form. It means nothing less than the intervention of God in our midst to do the unthinkable and impossible. But He has done it, and still continues to be able to do it for us wherever we will let Him work and take control. And when we experience how marvellously He can do it and has done it, then we begin to see that other lesser miracles are also possible with Him, and we look forward beyond death to the glorious restoration of all things in which He will complete what He has already begun.

THE STILLING OF THE STORM

On that day, when evening had come, he said to them, "Let us go across to the other side." And leaving the crowd, they took him with them, just as he was, in the boat. And other boats were with him. And a great storm of wind arose, and the waves beat into the boat, so that the boat was already filling. But he was in the stern, asleep on the cushion; and they woke him and said to him, "Teacher, do you not care if we perish?" And he awoke and rebuked the wind, and said to the sea, "Peace! Be still!" And the wind ceased, and there was a great calm. He said to them, "Why are you afraid? Have you no faith?" And they were filled with awe, and said to one another, "Who then is this, that even wind and sea obey him?"

Mk. IV. 35-41.

Most of us at some time or other have to admit that our greatest weakness lies in our lack of faith. If we had more of it, our lives would be different. This is often our chief problem in life.

This story can help us, for it shows how weak was the faith even of these disciples who by this time had come under Jesus's influence so much that they had left all and followed Him. Here we see their faith tested, and shown up, like ours, in all its frailty. We also learn where the danger lies, and where the cure can be found.

FEAR OVERCOMING FAITH

"On that day, when evening had come, he said to them, 'Let us go across to the other side.' And leaving the crowd, they took him with them, just as he was, in the boat."

This was the hour of trial for their faith. Humanly speaking there was real danger. If Jesus had not been responsible for this journey and its outcome, the situation would have been critical indeed. Peter and James and John and the other disciples were experienced fishermen, hardened to the wind and the storm. They knew this lake with all its treacherous moods and currents. They knew well what little chance a boat like theirs had when the storm reached the point at which it was then raging. They became really afraid—for they could not hope to survive a storm like this.

57

But Jesus the Lord, in whose word they had put their trust was with them in this boat that was so direly threatened. They were therefore faced with a simple and challenging choice: Were they going to behave as if His presence counted for nothing? In their view of things every kind of unruliness and disorder in this world was due to evil demonic forces. Disease, fever and madness were all caused by devils. This storm was no less caused by devils. But they had already seen Jesus controlling disease, fever and madness, and rebuking the devils for causing such things. Were they now going to believe that Jesus was Lord over the power of this storm, or were they going to allow their minds and hearts to become possessed by the fear that the evil power of the storm, and not Jesus, could ultimately decide the outcome of this voyage?

In this situation their weak faith failed, and they gave first place to fear rather than to Christ. They, who had previously committed so much of their minds' and hearts' devotion to Christ, now succumbed to the storm.

Christ's very presence in the boat with them should have set their minds completely at rest, but they allowed the storm to enter their minds and to crush out even the possibility of such confidence. It is true that in their fear they prayed to the sleeping Christ and aroused Him to help them. But even that was a prayer inspired by fear of the storm rather than by faith in Him. Fear had overcome faith. They had given way in the midst of what was not simply a critical earthly situation but rather a severe and vital and spiritual conflict. They had let fear and the storm paralyse their faith. That is why they were rebuked by Jesus. *"Why are you afraid? Have you no faith?"* Fear had been lord where He should have been given the Lordship.

We are all in the midst of this same intense, critical, spiritual battle. The New Testament is sterner than we at first would like to think in warning us against giving way to fear. Our Lord Himself made it one of His commandments that we should resist fear by faith. "Let not your hearts be troubled, believe in God, believe also in me," He said to His disciples, and again He repeated it to them. "Let not your hearts be troubled neither let them be afraid" (Jn. xiv. 1, 27). Paul, too, warns us about the "spirit of timidity" (ii Tim. i. 7) or the "spirit of slavery" which makes men "fall back into fear" (Rom. viii. 15), and

John reminds us that fear is to be "cast out" of our lives by "perfect love" (1 Jn. IV. 18). As we are commanded to love, we are thus equally commanded not to fear. In the sombre catalogue in the book of Revelation describing the damned who are excluded from eternal blessedness, John lists the "cowardly and faithless" in front of, and along with, murderers, fornicators, idolaters and other such like (Rev. XXI. 8). We know, too, from life itself, that once men and women begin to allow themselves to be motivated by fear, to the exclusion of love and gratitude, there is no end to the baseness and devastation that can ensue. The fight of faith against fear in the life of all of us is therefore of vital importance. Woe to us if, like the disciples, we ever become possessed by fear.

The situation in which we have to choose whether we are going to give first place either to fear or faith within our hearts is one into which we will be often brought if we follow Jesus Christ. It is important to note that it was Jesus Christ Himself who led His disciples into this situation that night, for He asked them to go that way at that very time. Today He treats us as He treated them, leads us as He led them, puts us through it as He put them through it. Why should we expect it otherwise? This is why the Christian life, and Christian service, is full of critical experiences in which our main struggle is to look to Christ always in order to overcome the fear that would paralyse faith.

Faith overcoming Fear

In the midst of this terrifying storm, up till the moment when they rudely awakened Him, Jesus was lying in the boat, sound asleep. He had been utterly weary. He had toiled for days amongst the crowds, spending Himself in an almost ceaseless round of preaching and healing in His ministry to the poor and sick and hungry. This journey in the boat had been for Him a needed escape for rest. He had deliberately laid Himself down and had slept on peacefully all through what were for the disciples fearful hours of ordeal and defeat in their battle with fear and the fierce elements. And there He was still sleeping, still even imperturbed! They could stand it no more and they shook Him and cried out in reproach and desperation, "*Teacher, do you not care if we perish?*"

This contrast between the slumbering peaceful Christ and the tormented fearful disciples must raise in our minds the question —what makes the great difference? Why did Jesus remain so steadfast and utterly courageous, while all the others gave way so recklessly to fear? Why is it that one man in the hour of real peril can remain so calm and confident while everyone else is in terror? What is it that can thus enable a man to find rest for his soul in the midst of a world so full of turmoil and chaos? The answer is found in Jesus's own confession of His secret. "And He who sent me is with me; He has not left me alone, for I always do what is pleasing to Him" (Jn. viii. 29).

Faith had overcome fear. He rested His soul in the Father-hood of God. He knew that His Father had always directed His life and guided His plans. This journey was therefore part of His Father's plan. His Father knew and cared. He knew that His Father had work for Him to do. Therefore His Father would preserve Him body and soul till His work on earth was done, and then He would have a work and place for Him in Heaven. He knew that He was on His Father's business. Therefore His safety was His Father's business. He knew that He needed sleep. Without it He could not physically carry on His work. Therefore He would lie down in peace and sleep, for His God would make Him to dwell in safety.

Christ is our Lord, and is therefore different from us. Every-thing that applies to Him does not always apply to us. But in this respect He is meant to be our example. "As the Father has loved me, so have I loved you" (Jn. xv. 9). In this we are meant to look to Him as He looked to the Father. If the disciples had even begun to reason with themselves, as Christ reasoned on that night, they would not have feared. If only they had remembered that it was He who had been responsible for bring-ing them out on the lake that night, and that He had never yet planned anything badly, they would have quietly waited for Him to act.

Moreover our behaviour in the critical moments of life is determined, more than we realise, by what is habitual with us in our day-to-day life. Whether we know where to look, whither to turn, how to keep our mind and heart calm, when the storms arise and the waves threaten, depends on where we look and whither we turn in gratitude and faith as each ordinary day arises and each ordinary occasion comes to pass. But it was because He always looked to the Father, whatever His circumstances, and did those things that pleased Him, that in this hour of crisis it was simply natural for Him to be calm and peaceful. This kind of faith that teaches us to look constantly to Him in all things, and that lives by what it finds in this looking, can make all the differences in our lives—the difference between the sleeping Christ and the fearful terrified disciples. It is significant that after those men came to know Christ better, and learned more of what it meant to walk with Him, they learned how faith overcomes fear and gives rest. We can think of Peter, after the resurrection, thrown into prison, condemned to die the next day, and "the very night when Herod was about to bring him out, Peter was sleeping between the soldiers, bound with two chains" (Acts XII. 6). He has learned by this time how faith can overcome fear. "He gives to His beloved sleep" (Ps. CXXVII. 2).

THE WORD THAT CREATES FAITH AND CONTROLS FEAR

"And he awoke and rebuked the wind, and said to the sea, Peace! Be still!"

When they heard Him rebuking the wind with His voice, they would remember how they had also heard Him rebuking the devils and fevers with His voice. And His Word was with power. *"And the wind ceased and there was a great calm."* His Word controlled the winds and the waves as it had controlled the devils and the fevers and death itself. It had authority over the huge and unruly forces of nature, as it had had authority over the diseases and disorders of the social life of man. He not only rebuked with His Word the winds of the air and the waves of the sea that day, He rebuked also by the same Word the winds and waves of fear in the hearts of the disciples. Having quelled the storms, He now turned to them and said *"Why are you afraid? Have you no faith?"* Indeed, the main point in this miracle story is not so much the power of His rebuke on the raging sea, as the power of His rebuke on the terror in the hearts of His disciples. His Word controlled their fear, and created faith.

The disciples in the lake are by no means alone in experiencing this miracle of the power of Jesus. "My sheep hear my voice," He said (Jn. X. 27). He promised that every age would be able to hear the same voice which calmed the waves and the disciples on the lake. Many miracles of grace take place in the Church today as we offer through Word and Sacrament our worship to God. One of the greatest is that through the Scripture read and preached we hear this powerful living voice of Jesus Christ which in the midst of all the problems and struggles of our human life today can subdue our wild passions, and can give us the inward peace that alone can make us sane and ordered in our living. Listening to His voice, we must let His Word quell every unruly thing within us—not only our fears but also our envyings and angers and covetings and lusts. It is not in our self-mastery, but in the faith that comes through hearing the Word of God, that we find the secret of true self-control.

Moreover let us have faith that the living Word of Christ can today control not only the storms of fear and passion within our individual hearts, but also, if men will listen to Him, the deep-seated disorders that throw societies and nations into unruliness and conflict. In several places in the Bible the restless and sinful world in its wickedness is likened to the raging and wild sea (Dan. VII. 2; Rev. XIII. 1; Is. LVII. 20). It is of the utmost social significance that at the heart of the Gospel, the Christ who speaks His Word is shown forth as the One who has power to rule and control the raging of the sea and to still the storms amongst the nations when these arise.

The Majesty and Lowliness of Him who speaks

The disciples were convinced that no ordinary being could utter such a Word as Jesus uttered in the boat that night. *"And they were filled with awe and said one to another, 'Who then is this, that even wind and sea obey Him?'"* They were familiar with the old Testament, and they knew that only the Lord Himself could thus rule the raging of the waves and the tumult of the sea (Ps. LXXXIX. 9, CVII. 23–30). Indeed, their minds were bound to think back on how the Word of the living God had controlled the sea to save Israel His people in the days of the Exodus from Egypt. And perhaps also they thought of how in the beginning the Word of God the Creator brought order out of chaos in creating this world. Did not this man speak the same almighty, creative, redeeming Word of God? And yet He who spoke this word was certainly also a man like themselves, who shortly before had been so tired He could hold up His head no longer, and had sunk into sleep from sheer human exhaustion, a man who was so human as to be genuinely surprised and grieved that His trusted friends should so mistrust Him. Yet He can now rise up in all His majesty, and at His voice the waves are still!

True God and True man! This is who He was and this is who He always is. In Him, God in all reality took upon Himself our human nature and became as we are. And yet in so emptying Himself He did not cease at the same time to be the Lord of all. And still today, even in the midst of the glory to which He has returned, He does not cease to be the man who can understand and sympathise with all our frailty, with all our nervousness and fears in the midst of our present storms.

"*They were filled with awe.*" This is the true fear of God that we must seek, and indeed cultivate, as we progress in the Christian life. It is a fear which, when we are given to experience it, can indeed drive out of us all our other faithless and cowardly fears. And when we allow this true fear to be born and grow within us, we find ourselves also more and more trusting in God's Fatherhood, and we become afraid of nothing else on earth "And do not fear those who kill the body but cannot kill the soul: rather fear Him who can destroy both soul and body in hell. Are not two sparrows sold for a penny? And not one of them will fall to the ground without your Father's will. But even the hairs of your head are all numbered. Fear not, therefore; you are of more value than many sparrows" (Mt. x. 28–31).

THE GADARENE DEMONIAC

They came to the other side of the sea, to the country of the Gerasenes. And when he had come out of the boat, there met him out of the tombs a man with an unclean spirit, who lived among the tombs; and no one could bind him any more, even with a chain; for he had often been bound with fetters and chains, but the chains he wrenched apart, and the fetters he broke in pieces; and no one had the strength to subdue him. Night and day among the tombs and on the mountains he was always crying out, and bruising himself with stones. And when he saw Jesus from afar, he ran and worshiped him; and crying out with a loud voice, he said, "What have you to do with me, Jesus, Son of the Most High God? I adjure you by God, do not torment me." For he had said to him, "Come out of the man, you unclean spirit!" And Jesus asked him, "What is your name?" He replied, "My name is Legion; for we are many." And he begged him eagerly not to send them out of the country. Now a great herd of swine was feeding there on the hillside; and they begged him, "Send us to the swine, let us enter them." So he gave them leave. And the unclean spirits came out, and entered the swine; and the herd, numbering about two thousand, rushed down the steep bank into the sea, and were drowned in the sea.

The herdsmen fled, and told it in the city and in the country. And people came to see what it was that had happened. And they came to Jesus, and saw the demoniac sitting there, clothed and in his right mind, the man who had had the legion; and they were afraid. And those who had seen it told what had happened to the demoniac and to the swine. And they began to beg Jesus to depart from their neighborhood. And as he was getting into the boat, the man who had been possessed with demons begged him that he might be with him. But he refused, and said to him, "Go home to your friends, and tell them how much the Lord has done for you, and how he has had mercy on you." And he went away and began to proclaim in the Decapolis how much Jesus had done for him; and all men marveled.

Mk. v. 1–20.

An unchanging Social problem

On a first reading we are tempted to dismiss this story as one having very little to say to our modern world. It seems to relate to a remote, simple and primitive age. In Gadara in those days, the local banker was the swineherd, and a man's wealth was reckoned by the number of pigs that belonged to him. Naked

64

madmen were allowed to roam the countryside, menacing the public, living in tombs, and finding their amusement by cutting themselves with sharp stones. We are bound to wonder whether the world to which this kind of thing belongs has anything in common with an age like our own.

But the more we think it over, the more we find that there is a deep underlying similarity between that primitive world with its crude problems and our own. One of the greatest problems confronting society in every age is that of how to control the wild elements in man's common nature which tend to defy control and try to express themselves in contempt of law and order, and in acts of violence and indecency and unruliness. In these days in Gadara this disordered spirit of lawlessness found its expression in the brutal and stupid behaviour of these demoniacs. Today the same deep-rooted perversion of the human mind and heart and nature expresses itself in more apparently civilised and better dressed forms. It expresses itself sometimes in mass hysteria, sometimes in mob violence, sometimes in waves of juvenile delinquency or anti-semitism. Sometimes it ultimately finds its expression in the determination of a nation, fascinated and led by disordered minds, to wage war and work havoc on the earth in pursuit of wild and senseless ambition.

We are reminded at the start of this story that the use of force by civil government gives no ultimate and lasting solution to the problem. The Gadarene demoniac who was such a problem *"lived among the tombs; and no one could bind him any more, even with a chain; for he had often been bound with fetters and chains, but the chains he wrenched apart, and the fetters he broke in pieces; and no one had the strength to subdue him."* The civil authorities of Gadara had done their best to maintain public order and decency by force. They reinforced the police, forged the strongest possible chains, issued the strictest instructions, but the situation was beyond their control. Each time new and stronger chains were tried they worked only for a very short time and the disorder broke out afresh.

Today it is the same story. As the wave of crime and violence mounts we are apt to think that severe legal penalties are a real solution. We strengthen the police force, tighten the regulations, and lengthen prison sentences in an attempt to stamp out the violence, indecency and hooliganism. All this may be necessary. Many people in addition feel that the best antidote to crimes of violence is the reintroduction of corporal punishment in our prisons. The tragedy is that by themselves such measures do not solve the problem. The stronger the chains we apply the more disappointing the final result is apt to be, for we are here dealing with something that cannot be permanently chained. And the more brutal the punishment, the more brutal is apt to be the final reaction of the criminal when the chain is snapped and opportunity comes. This disorder has roots too deep and is of too subtle and complex a nature to be amenable to a treatment that involves force alone. This is why prominent cabinet ministers realising the limitations of legislation and force, have appealed time and again to the Church for help to solve a problem that they recognise as too deep-seated for any civil authority finally to cope with.

The underlying Cause

The people of Gadara like everyone else in Jesus's time, were sure that they knew the underlying cause of these vexing disorders that were troubling their social life. They were certain that the men who did such violent and indecent things were possessed by demons. To them earth's life was touched at every point by the life of two other realms, one of which was full of devils who could interfere with everything that goes on here. They could cause physical disease and accidents. They could possess people and split up their personality and make them mad and invite them to commit suicide. "They sat on thrones, they hovered around cradles. The earth was literally a hell, though it continued to be a creation of God." These simple people had no doubt that it was the demons that caused not only the wild behaviour of the possessed man in this story, but also the mad rush of the swine to their own self-destruction.

Today most of us are not so sure about the details of the working of evil powers in this world. We know that many of the physical diseases that originally were attributed to devils can be cured by ordinary medicine, that some of the nervous and mental illnesses which our forefathers put down to Satanic causes, can be cured by physical or psychological treatment. Moreover, the average man today finds the very idea that there exists a multitude of individual devils able to possess personalities a very difficult one to hold. As Leslie Weatherhead writes, "The idea that the human personality can be possessed by demons is widely rejected today by the educated westerner as an outworn superstition. Evidence and symptoms which to the easterner of the old days pointed to demon possession are either dismissed as unfactual, or explained in terms of nervous or hysterical illness. The modern man has no place for demons, and when he reads, in a passage in St. Mark's Gospel . . . that a demon 'dasheth him down: and he foameth and grindeth with his teeth and pineth away' the modern man murmurs, 'Epilepsy' with a superiority which, he assumes, leaves no questions unanswered.''

But the fact that we cannot now attribute certain particular illnesses to the possession of individual men by demons does not mean that this story has not a profound lesson to teach us about what lies at the root of all these deep-rooted disorders of society of which we have been speaking. Jesus acted on the assumption that this man was possessed by devils. He acted as if He believed that evil powers could possess men. Some of His most stern words are a warning to Simon Peter that Satan was seeking to possess him, and a warning to us that if we do not allow His Spirit fully to possess our hearts, they will become occupied by evil spirits (Lk. xxii. 31; Mt. xii. 45). In all these actions and sayings, He is setting the seal of His authority on the vivid language and beliefs of the people around Him, and using that language to warn us about a terrible fate and reality that can destroy our souls and our bodies and our society unless we take His warning. And if He could find no better way and no better language to use in pointing to this terrible reality that is behind our social unruliness, then if we believe in Him, we should not be ashamed to use it and say we believe also that devils are real, and can be a real and root cause of our social misery, our moral chaos and the pernicious outbreaks of unruly passion that arise among men and nations. What took place in Germany under Hitler helped afresh to convince many people that demonic powers are still active in this modern world and can take possession of nations and their rulers if they lay themselves open to their influence. And what still takes place today in the mission fields, where the Church confronts heathenism in its crudest forms, convinces missionaries that only some theory of devil-possession is adequate to account for the kind of conflict in which they become involved. Dr. Weatherhead further writes that "after certain observations in the East, wide enquiry from scholars, and such study as I have been able to pursue during the last thirty years" he is certain of one thing, that no one can dismiss stories of demon-possession in a light-hearted way. There are, moreover, many ordinary people whose experience at times in situations that can arise in ordinary life must convince them in their own minds that the demons are by no means a superstition of the past at which we can afford to smile too much.

Therefore, though details in this story may tend to offend us, let us not be too wise to learn what it has to teach us. Certainly Jesus, in this incident, may have been to an extent accommodating His actions to the ideas of the poor heathen people He was confronting in this backward area. When He asked the demons their name, He seems to have been using the well-known technique that was expected of the expert exorcists of His day when they were called in to cast out devils. He, no doubt, did this to give the man confidence. It is possible, too, that He deliberately made the destruction of the swine a sign to the poor bewildered sufferer that he had indeed been cured— after all, His own teaching is that a man is of much more value than anything in the animal creation (Lk. XII. 24).

But, however we may interpret these details, when we look at what is central and essential in the teaching of this incident we are brought face to face with the basic problem of human life. The task to which Jesus dedicated His whole life for men was not simply that of overcoming a purely human defect in attitude of heart and mind towards God, nor was it only that of cancelling the fate into which man had been caught up through his guilt before God. The task we see Jesus fulfilling all through His life was that delivering men from powers and forces greater than themselves, of fighting and overcoming and casting out from the midst of human affairs the powers of darkness that have held mankind in terrible bondage and corruption and disorder. These powers have suffered their final and decisive defeat through the intervention of His human life, culminating in His victory on the Cross and Resurrection. But they are still alive and still powerfully active in our midst today, and will be till Christ comes again. That is why we must watch and pray and fight them. Therefore when we face the tasks we have to do today in the name of Jesus, we would do well to see them in the light of the revelation He has given us of their real and fundamental nature.

THE ETERNAL CHOICE FACING SOCIETY

Jesus proved Himself the complete master of the evil powers that were disturbing the Gadarene countryside. The story is ludicrous, and is meant to be so. Seeing there was a great herd of swine, the devils begged Jesus not to send them out of the country but to let them go into the swine. "*So he gave them leave. And the unclean spirits came out, and entered into the swine, and the herd, numbering about two thousand, rushed down the steep bank into the sea, and were drowned in the sea.*" The point in the story is obviously that Jesus solved this problem with perfect ease. He completely outwitted all the devils and made them seem utterly foolish. Evil has no real power or initiative when Jesus Christ comes on the scene. He has come to destroy the works of the devil. Therefore by a mere word He accomplishes what the local government with all their chains and police are unable to do. They come on the scene to find the most terrifying problem "*sitting there, clothed and in his right mind.*" No fear of any more gangsterdom or indecency in this region.

The Word of Christ has the same power today. "You are the salt of the earth" (Mt. v. 13), said Jesus once to His disciples. Salt stays corruption. It prevents disintegration and rottenness. Jesus means that His Church by its presence and example and by its proclamation of the Word of Christ shall be able to restrain the forces of evil within a community and prevent society from succumbing to disorder and corruption. The Word of Christ today can subdue lawlessness. A wise government will always recognise the restraining and moral power of the Word of the Lord, and will encourage and support the Church as it seeks to subdue the hearts of men and women, young and old to Him who speaks in its midst today with this living power. For where there is no Word of Christ, there are only two other alternatives. Either to allow lawless forces to terrify and corrupt, or to forge stronger and stronger chains to be applied with more and more brutality by a larger and larger police force—and thus you have the development of society into a tyranny or a totalitarian state. Jesus Christ alone can offer the one restraining force that can prevent lawlessness and yet preserve true liberty by avoiding such totalitarianism. "Where the Spirit of the Lord is, there is freedom" (II Cor. III. 17).

But sometimes it appears to be a costly and dangerous thing for members of a nation or community to allow Christ complete freedom to speak His Word in their midst, and each society has to choose whether or not it wants to be involved in such danger and such cost. When Jesus cast out the devils in Gadara He caused an unparalleled commotion and a public scandal. His experiment cost a whole herd of swine. The people and their leaders felt that this was too high a price to pay for order and decency. They shuddered at the thought of what might happen were they to allow Him to tackle any more of the problems that existed in their public life. They were faced with the choice, either to go on suffering the disturbance caused by devils, or to allow themselves to disturbed in a different way by Jesus. They chose on the spot, without any attempt at compromise. *"They began to beg Jesus to depart from their neighbourhood."* It is possible, too, of course, that they believed the devils might somehow work some revenge if they kept Him in their midst.

We must face the cost, and choose to be disturbed, if we wish to have Jesus Christ in our midst. He sometimes creates a greater disturbance than is involved by leaving evil at peace and things as they are. When Jesus cured the possessed, before the devils came out of their victims they often threw them into fierce convulsions and they became extremely noisy. When Jesus cleansed the temple, He plunged the whole place into an uproar and upset the local traders. His own description of the effect His teaching will have on homes and society is, surely, enough to make us think twice about the worth-whileness of letting Him have His way. "Do you think that I have come to give peace on earth? No, I tell you, but rather division; for henceforth in one house there will be five divided, three against two and two against three; they will be divided, father against son and son against father, mother against daughter and daughter against her mother" (Lk. XII. 51–3). His description of the signs that will appear on earth as His Kingdom is more and more allowed to develop and grow, are nearly all signs of profound disturbance and upheaval. A community that allows Christ and His Kingdom freedom in its midst will be one in which all the proud and greedy and sordid elements which are found in every human society will never be allowed to settle down in peace, but will be continually tormented and challenged by the Word of God. Therefore there will be constant tension and trouble in its midst. But at the same time there will be a new kind of peace and stability through the constantly recurring victory of Christ's Word over the "unfruitful works of darkness" (Eph. v. 11).

CHRIST LEAVES HIS WITNESS

Whatever choice society may make officially with respect to Jesus Christ does not, however, alter the responsibility of the individual Christian. The man of Gadara who was cured so miraculously wanted now to flee from his pagan environment. As Jesus was getting into the boat *"he begged him that he might be with him."* But Jesus refused to take him away. *"Go home to your friends,"* He said, *"and tell them how much the Lord has done for you, and how he has had mercy on you."* Here is where our service of the Lord must begin. How simple and natural it is that a man under such circumstances should first go home and share what has come to him with those who are nearest to him in kinship, and that like Matthew, the publican, he should gather his friends together to rejoice with him. And yet the healed man never thought of doing so, and Jesus had to tell him to go and do it.

This is, moreover, the kind of witness that no amount of official disapproval of the Gospel of Christ can effectively stop. From all over the world today we hear now and then of fresh official barriers and difficulties put here and there in the way of the Church's advance or even of the Church's normal routine of teaching the young in the faith. But Jesus Christ cannot be entirely shut out. By means of the simple and natural process of one man telling his friends and neighbours He can retain His hold where He has once set His feet.

It is a remarkable fact that this nervous man, who had wanted to flee from the country soon found himself involved in a ministry and a mission that had a great effect, not simply among his kith and kin and friends, but also amongst the whole community in which he lived. *"And he went away, and began to proclaim in the Decapolis how much Jesus had done for him; and all men marveled."*

THE RAISING OF JAIRUS'S DAUGHTER

And when Jesus had crossed again in the boat to the other side, a great crowd gathered about him; and he was beside the sea. Then came one of the rulers of the synagogue, Jairus by name; and seeing him, he fell at his feet, and besought him, saying, "My little daughter is at the point of death. Come and lay your hands on her, so that she may be made well, and live." And he went with him.

And a great crowd followed him and thronged about him. And there was a woman who had had a flow of blood for twelve years, and who had suffered much under many physicians, and had spent all that she had, and was no better but rather grew worse. She had heard the reports about Jesus, and came up behind him in the crowd and touched his garment. For she said, "If I touch even his garments, I shall be made well." And immediately the haemorrhage ceased; and she felt in her body that she was healed of her disease. And Jesus, perceiving in himself that power had gone forth from him, immediately turned about in the crowd, and said, "Who touched my garments?" And his disciples said to him, "You see the crowd pressing around you, and yet you say, 'Who touched me?'" And he looked around to see who had done it. But the woman, knowing what had been done to her, came in fear and trembling and fell down before him, and told him the whole truth. And he said to her, "Daughter, your faith has made you well; go in peace, and be healed of your disease."

While he was still speaking, there came from the ruler's house some who said, "Your daughter is dead. Why trouble the Teacher any further?" But ignoring what they said, Jesus said to the ruler of the synagogue, "Do not fear, only believe." And he allowed no one to follow him except Peter and James and John the brother of James. When they came to the house of the ruler of the synagogue, he saw a tumult, and people weeping and wailing loudly. And when he had entered, he said to them, "Why do you make a tumult and weep? The child is not dead but sleeping." And they laughed at him. But he put them all outside, and took the child's father and mother and those who were with him, and went in where the child was. Taking her by the hand he said to her, "Talitha cumi"; which means, "Little girl, I say to you, arise." And immediately the girl got up and walked; for she was twelve years old. And immediately they were overcome with amazement. And he strictly charged them that no one should know this, and told them to give her something to eat.

Mk. v. 21–43.

"AND HE WENT WITH HIM"

In this miracle story we see Jesus going home with a man who has come to seek His help. It did not always happen in this way. Many miracle stories tell how the patient was carried to Him, or came to Him, or met Him on the road as if by accident. Other miracle stories tell of how Jesus cured from a distance people who were ill at home, without Himself going near them. In this instance, however, He was begged by a man to go to his house where his little daughter lay critically ill. Jairus the ruler of the synagogue in his agony over the apparently hopeless illness that had seized his little one, pushed his way through the great crowd gathered by the seaside to hear Jesus, and was bold enough to beg Him to interrupt His teaching of the great multitude in order to come home with him to see what He could do. And Jesus *"went with him"* in spite of the fact that a huge crowd was there waiting for His ministry. It was a sad and anxious journey that they took together, towards a home that had been darkened with a great sorrow.

The fact that Jesus went home with Jairus on this journey has a deep and significant meaning for all who have such journeys home to make, and such problems to face there as Jairus had to face. We often think with gladness of the wonderful reality of Christ's presence with us here in the Church. He comes here to meet us and to speak with us. We believe He has something to say to us and to give us here—vision, inspiration, forgiveness, and strength. If we have grasped this, and have really met Him and listened to Him and prayed to Him in this place, then we are happy indeed. But far too many people think of Church-going as leading to one "brief, bright, hour of fellowship" with Christ that soon passes, and then we leave with nothing but an impression and a memory. There is something else that we yet have to discover. He comes here not only to be able to meet us for a "brief, bright hour," but also in order to be able to go with us. He is here so that we can ask Him to accompany us on our way home, and on our way into the midst of our trials and anxieties and temptations as He accompanied Jairus.

This is why at the centre of the Christian faith we have not only the cradle in which He was born, but also the Cross, to which He spent all His life travelling. The Christmas cradle means that God has come to meet us. He has come from heaven to earth, right into the midst of our human life. He was born a babe in a manger so that we can come and meet Him and adore Him. But the Cross means even more than the cradle. The Cross means that God comes into this world not just to make it possible for us to meet Him but in order to go with us all the way we have to go. It means that when God came into this human life in Jesus Christ He came not simply to enter its top and sublime levels, not simply to enter its Churches and temples and good religious circles where men come to meet God and to be at their best, but He came also in order to be able to go down all the avenues of our life, no matter how low these lead into sordidness, sin, bitterness and death. It was on His journey from the cradle to the Cross that He went with people to such places as the homes of publicans and sinners, of proud pharisees like Simon, and of broken-hearted Jairus.

He will go with us as far as we have to go. He will go home with us whatever be the problem that faces us there, the tragedy that hovers there or the threat that broods there. He will not even draw the line at going with us to the office or the factory or the shop on Monday morning. There is no place into which we have to go, that is too dubious or mundane or sordid for Him also, who started at the cradle and finished up in apparent God-forsakenness on the Cross. When Jairus came to Him and asked Him to come home, He asked no question about the situation there, or the goings-on there. He laid down no conditions. He knew only that there was a sad and critical situation, and He *"went with him."*

JESUS RESCUES JAIRUS'S FAITH

It was faith that had brought Jairus to Jesus. He believed that this Teacher and Healer could do something for him in his need and despair. It must have given him an encouraging thrill in his effort of faith, to find that Jesus was willing to leave the crowd to go with him.

But very soon he found that faith, instead of remaining a thrill, became a hard and grim battle against the world and against despair—a battle in which he could not have survived for a moment unless Jesus had been with him.

There was first of all a tormenting delay. They started off towards his house and he had to battle with fear that already they might be too late. But just when he began to feel there was perhaps a good chance, a woman came up to Jesus in the crowd, and caused a stir and held Him up, by touching Him for healing and drawing off His attention. And Jesus had to waste time in attending to her.

And then at this critical time when his faith was beginning to wilt, there came the cry, "Why trouble to go on any further?" Some of his friends had been at the house. And their report was that the child was dead and it was too late and it seemed sensible to them to come and stop him from bringing this Teacher all the way now. "*There came from the ruler's house some who said, 'Your daughter is dead. Why trouble the teacher any further?'*"

These were wise sane men, full of common sense. This was their considered opinion, for they wanted to help him. And this considered opinion of these wise sane practical decent men was calculated to shatter his last shred of hope and faith, and to put him for ever off the track he had started on with Jesus. And their advice was so sensible that he would now be holding himself up for ridicule if he did not take it. Why continue stupidly to hope? Why not now face up to the finality of the world's practical judgment, and the reality of death, when death is death? If Jesus had not been with him this would have been the end of all hope for Jairus.

But now a wonderful thing happened. Jesus stepped in to interfere and rescue Jairus's faith from being destroyed by the world's common sense and sanity. A battle began, a battle for faith against sensible decent public opinion. "*Ignoring what they said, Jesus said to the ruler of the synagogue, 'Do not fear, only believe'.*"

Jairus is told to ignore common sense, sanity, the wisdom of all his friends. "*Do not fear, only believe.*"

Who is he to listen to? To which word has he to give place in his heart?

Has he to listen to these words of the wisdom of the world? "*Trouble not the Master any further.* Resign yourself Jairus. Face up to life with all its stark realities, and with all the possibilities it holds of failure and death. Face it bravely and squarely. If you have had it, you have had it, and you must take it like a man. This is a world where miracles such as you are hoping for do not happen, where religion has to be given a place, but kept in its place. Push this thing no further."

Or has he to listen to this strange and wonderful man who has already inspired so much trust and said so much to give him this faith, who has spoken so much about the power of faith, and who is there beside him inspiring him to keep going on, and to keep on believing saying, "*Do not fear. Only believe.*"

Do we not understand this battle? And have we not been in it? Perhaps, indeed, we are right in the midst of it even today. We too have our visions and hopes raised in us by Jesus Christ, especially when He speaks to us in the Church about what He can do for us and with us, now and into eternity. We too have our thrilling starts on the fresh journey into life with Jesus from the door of the Church. We are going to start again. "If any one is in Christ, he is new creation; the old has passed away, behold, the new has come" (II Cor. v. 17). That is what we believe can happen to us. From henceforth we are going to live by a faith that can make all things new.

But we do not have to travel far even from the Church door on a Sunday morning before it meets us—the sane, practical, reasonable, decent, commercial, calculating world. It meets us even at Church, or it comes to tea on Sundays and incidentally keeps us from coming back to Church. Its common-sense philosophy is implied in every remark that is made to us—especially if we let it be known that something in Church has given us new hope and life. "Trouble not yourself my dear fellow. Don't let foolish thoughts unsettle you. Keep your feet very much on the ground, for there are no wings by which any man can rise any higher, or become sure of anything beyond the finality of the grave, the importance of money, and the common sense of having a good time here without too much excess. Dreaming dreams and seeing vision beyond all this will never get anyone anywhere." The Bible speaks of this present evil world from which Jesus Christ has come to deliver us (Gal. i. 14). This dangerous world does not always meet us in the form of dubious dance halls and entertainments, gambling dens and drinking parlours. It can meet us also with its terrible challenge in the guise of so many decent, practical common-sense friends. Even they can present us with a front line where we must fight the good fight of faith.

But Jesus made sure that He was going to win this battle to give Jairus the freedom to believe. He pushed the world with its common sense and sanity right out of reach. *"He allowed no one to follow him except Peter and James and John the brother of James."* And when they arrived at the house there was another enemy to face. There were the mourners filling the place with dismal sounds of gloom. Some of them had been hired for the job and were experts at tearing their hair and beating their breasts and wailing piteously. Some of them were friends, neighbours and relatives who had come to help in the performance of the last rites.

But such gloom is no atmosphere for a home in which Jesus Christ is to work miracles of new life and resurrection. And it was as great a menace to Jairus's faith as the practical advice of His friends. And Jesus began to attack this too in His battle for the soul and faith of Jairus. Ruthlessly He put the whole crowd outside. *"Why do you make a tumult and weep? The child is not dead but sleeping."* And then they revealed the sinister and deadly nature of their gloom by laughing not at Jairus but at Him. *"They laughed at him."*

We are tempted often to give way to gloom, to sink in it, to let it fill our homes. How pervasive and infectious it is, and how quickly it spreads and settles down everywhere if we give it entrance. But we must learn to regard gloom as a poison to faith, and as something that seeks to exclude the power of Jesus Christ. This miracle story teaches us that the environment we choose to live in matters. Notice how Jesus cleared away from around Jairus everything harmful to his faith. He surrounded him with his own disciples. He spoke His word clearly, *"Do not fear, only believe."* *"The child is not dead, but sleeping."* He Himself stayed by him all the time. Let us allow Him to do the same for us. Let us allow Him to draw us again and again into the fellowship of the Church in which He seeks to give all of us the environment in which our faith can grow strong, in which we can constantly hear His assuring word spoken to us, in which He meets us again and again to set out with us afresh to where we have to go.

The Foretaste of the Power of His Resurrection

Into the home of Jairus, Jesus took not only sympathy, but also a foretaste of the power of His resurrection. He *"took the child's father and mother and those that were with him, and went in where the child was. Taking her by the hand he said to her, 'Talitha cumi", which means, 'Little girl, I say to you, arise.' And immediately the girl got up and walked; for she was twelve years old."*

His power to accomplish this miracle meant that the Resurrection power of the age-to-come was already there and then at work through the Word of Jesus. The Kingdom of God had indeed come with power and this miracle was a sign of its presence there in the home of Jairus. Today Jesus can bring the same resurrection power of the Kingdom into our own homes or our places of work whenever He enters them with us. His final proof that such power was no illusion or dream was His own Resurrection on the third day after they buried Him and sealed the tomb. We will not see the visible glory of this new Kingdom that is already in our midst till the day when Christ comes again in His glory. We do not need further visible proofs of its reality now that His own Resurrection has taken place. But we can know and experience its present power in our midst if we will let Him come with us into the situations in which we have so much need of His help.

It was Jairus's faith that was the key to the whole matter. In this miracle Jesus simply honoured the faith He had striven so much to keep alive in Jairus. Can we imagine that He would go so far with Jairus, do so much to give him hope, and then disappoint him? They will never be ashamed who trust in Him. The kind of hope we see in Jairus is the creation of Christ's Word, and is certain of its fulfilment.

Jairus's faith was not great and magnificent. It was little and weak. When he saw the miracle that this faith accomplished, he was *"overcome with amazement."* Faith is a strange thing. Even though it is often weak and sometimes almost perishing, it can at the same time be responsible for allowing Jesus Christ into life-situations in which He can do great things in the spread and manifestation of His glorious Kingdom. In this assurance lies not only salvation for us from the unbelieving world, but certain victory for us as we go out with our little faith to seek to conquer the unbelieving world in His name.

THE WOMAN WITH THE
FLOW OF BLOOD

And when Jesus had crossed again in the boat to the other side, a
great crowd gathered about him; and he was beside the sea. Then
came one of the rulers of the synagogue, Jairus by name; and seeing
him, he fell at his feet, and besought him, saying, "My little daughter
is at the point of death. Come and lay your hands on her, so that
she may be made well, and live." And he went with him.

And a great crowd followed him and thronged about him. And
there was a woman who had had a flow of blood for twelve years,
and who had suffered much under many physicians, and had spent
all that she had, and was no better but rather grew worse. She had
heard the reports about Jesus, and came up behind him in the crowd
and touched his garment. For she said, "If I touch even his garments, I shall be made well." And immediately the haemorrhage
ceased; and she felt in her body that she was healed of her disease.
And Jesus, perceiving in himself that power had gone forth from
him, immediately turned about in the crowd, and said, "Who
touched my garments?" And his disciples said to him, "You see the
crowd pressing around you, and yet you say, 'Who touched me?'"
And he looked around to see who had done it. But the woman,
knowing what had been done to her, came in fear and trembling
and fell down before him, and told him the whole truth. And he
said to her, "Daughter, your faith has made you well; go in peace,
and be healed of your disease."

Mk. v. 21–34.

Superficially, this woman was just one of the large crowd
that had gathered round Jesus. He was fairly popular at this
time. He had been doing many miracles, and the people enjoyed seeing such things done. He had been challenged publicly
by Scribes and Pharisees from Jerusalem and had answered
with skill and conviction. He was an interesting teacher
whom common people could listen to gladly. For these, and,
no doubt, other reasons, they thronged Him. This woman was
there amongst them. She looked one of the poorer class for she
was thin and ill-clad, having spent all her living on doctor's
fees over the past twelve years. Hers was indeed a weary and
exhausting sickness.

But below the surface, there was a world of difference in attitude and heart and in relationship to Jesus, between her and those who surrounded her. She alone, in her desperate faith, in the midst of this huge crowd that day made living contact with Jesus. She alone was healed and cleansed and blessed by Him. The people in the thronging crowds jostled Him. Many of them had some urgent need which He could have met by miraculous power had they had the faith of this poor woman. But though they heaved and pushed round Him nothing happened to them that changed their lives. This woman alone had the attitude towards Jesus which enabled Him to meet her human need. He did a miracle for her alone, for she alone touched Him with the touch that won blessing and salvation. As St. Augustine puts it, "Many thronged Him, one touched Him."

There has never been a time in history when Jesus Christ has not had some measure of popularity. As He gathered this crowd round Him in His journey through Galilee, so in His march down through the centuries He has always created the same kind of stir and drawn people round His Church in fairly large numbers. They still throng Him today. A Scottish quarterly Communion service, an Anglican Easter congregation or a special evangelistic effort such as a Billy Graham campaign, is a manifestation of the way in which people still crowd round Jesus Christ. But how many of us in this crowd round Jesus Christ today are merely thronging Him? And how many of us are really touching Him? There may be many whose names have been written on the roll of the Church, and who have thronged its services and yet have never in the midst of the throng put forth the hand of eager faith and made life-giving contact with the Lord Himself.

The presence of a crowd around Jesus does not necessarily mean that many miracles are taking place in the midst. Nor does our mere presence in the heart of the crowd mean that we are therefore at the heart of a living and powerful Christian influence. A great deal depends on the reason why we are there, and on our attitude and relationship to Him who is at the centre of the crowd.

The Faith that brought her into the Crowd

This woman was drawn into the heart of the crowd by a faith which, in a very vague way, recognised that Jesus Christ could meet her desperate need.

She had been almost driven to despair that her illness could ever be cured. She had tried every human source of help. For her there was only God left to turn to. Unless God helped her by a miracle there was no hope left.

But she heard of Jesus and she looked at Him. She must have watched Him at first from a distance. It seemed to her that a strange power must flow from His very body. Perhaps she watched Him on the day He cleansed the leper—or she had heard about it. He had stretched out His hand and touched the man saying, "Be clean" and immediately the leprosy had gone (Mk. i. 41). To her, there seemed to be a power to heal people in the very words He spoke, for He had sometimes only to speak a word and people when they heard it were cured. Nor did He always have to look up to heaven and pray, when He healed. He seemed to have this power in Himself, and when He gave it out, healings took place. She said to herself, "In Him there is the source of a divine power that can heal me. All I have to do is to get near enough to Him to be able to make some kind of contact with this power that overflows from Him, and it will cleanse my body."

She had seen, in the only way she could see it in her condition and circumstance, the heart of the Christian Gospel. The New Testament sometimes uses this woman's simple argument. It tells us that God has decided to give us everything we need to make our lives healthy and true and right and immortal in and through Jesus Christ. His human life was lived with a righteousness, wisdom, moral power and peace that are meant now to be our righteousness, wisdom, moral power and peace. All we have to do in order to receive these things from Him is to come to Him and enter life-giving communion with Him through faith. In this way everything that is His becomes ours. And this coming to Him by faith is not too difficult, for He comes into the midst where two or three gather together in His name. He comes near to us in such a way that we can enter this personal communion with Him and make contact with

Him as a spiritual presence. In this way our whole life in body and soul can become cleansed and made new. There is a key to the meaning of much that the New Testament says to us today, in this woman's simple yet profound insight. *"If I touch even his garments, I shall be made well."*

The Touch that brought Cleansing and Health

Once she had seen all this, and made her resolve to go near to Jesus and make contact with His life and power by touching His clothes, it was all very easy for the woman. She needed to do no more than mingle with the crowd, edge herself nearer and nearer, stretch out her hand to grip the corner of His robe with its tassels. He was there to touch.

The fact that He healed her in response to such a simple and straightforward touch means that He wants to encourage us to make the same approach to Himself today. He has made it as easy for us to touch Him today. It is true that He is no longer with us in bodily form for us to lay hold of His clothes as tangibly as did this woman. He has ascended beyond this world that we can touch and see, into a new sphere of glory and majesty. He warned His disciples that He was going to "go away" (Jn. xvi. 5–7) in this manner. But after He went away, He sent His spirit to take the place of His bodily presence, and He gave His disciples means and signs by which in every age we can be sure that we have His spiritual presence with all the life and power of His body in our midst. Indeed He has given us means by which we can enjoy the same "fellowship" with Him as they had who looked on Him with their eyes and touched Him with their hands (i Jn. i. 1–4). Through this "fellowship" we too can come as near to Him and make as close and powerful a life-giving contact with Him as this woman did in the midst of the crowd.

It is very significant that one of Jesus's first acts after His resurrection was to draw near to two of His disciples who were discussing Him on the road to Emmaus. First He made their hearts "burn within" them (Lk. xxiv. 32) as He spoke to them from the Bible, and then He made Himself "known to them in the breaking of the bread" as He sat at the supper table with them and took bread and blessed and broke it and gave it to them, as He had done at His last supper (Lk. xxiv. 30 and 35).

The risen Jesus deals with us in the same way today. As we gather together in the Church and the Scriptures are opened, and His Word is preached from them, He is there to be touched by our answering faith. He is there when the Lord's Supper is celebrated, in our midst in such a real way that as we stretch out our hands to take and handle the bread and wine so we can also stretch out the hand of our faith to touch His spiritual presence and enter that life-giving fellowship with Him that enables His power to cleanse and renew our lives.

We too need do no more than "touch" Him in this simple straightforward way and the whole of our need is met. *"She came up behind him in the crowd and touched his garments. . . . And immediately the haemorrhage ceased; and she felt in her body that she was healed of her disease."* The merest touch on her part did everything. She did not need to persuade Him, argue with Him, prove her worth or give her character. She would have been too timid, too dismayed and fearful to have ever come near Him, had she thought she needed to do that. And yet some of us today tend to keep ourselves away from Him because we feel that before we can get anything from Him, He will first require some sign of our worth or our sincerity or repentance. But this woman came to Him and touched Him just as she was, with her disease worse than it had ever been at any time in her life. And yet He did not shrink from her but healed her. His response to her is good news to us. Too many of us think that before He makes anything available for us we must on our part do something drastic and heroic to make ourselves a little better than we have been. But all that is required is the merest touch from us just as we are, even though we may feel worse than we have ever felt before. We need bring no guarantee for the future, no payment. He himself guarantees our future, and He Himself has paid all that is needed for what He will give us. His grace and love are there in Him waiting and eager to invade our lives with transforming power in response to the least sign on our part that we will have His gifts. The merest touch is enough. He is not such that His love and power need to be dragged out of Him or to be won from Him by those who first probe their source and sink a shaft deep into His heart.

This means, too, that before Christ gives Himself to us in His love and power there need be no great mental effort on our part to dig deep in the realms of Christian theology in order to come to a clear understanding of the main Christian doctrines. One of the beautiful features of this miracle is that at first this woman knew and understood very little. Her act of touching Him was at first an act of superstition as well as an act of faith, and He later corrects her for this. She did not properly understand what she was doing nor had she perhaps been near to Him before in her life. She did not know much about His being the Messiah of Israel. Her theology was summed up in one simple superstitious sentence, *"If I touch even his garments, I shall be made well,"* and He healed her.

THE INTERVIEW

Jesus was sensitive to her trembling touch in the midst of the thronging crowd. *"And Jesus, perceiving in himself that power had gone forth from him, immediately turned about in the crowd, and said, 'Who touched my garments?'"* His sensitiveness annoyed the disciples. *" 'You see the crowd pressing around you',"* they said, *" 'and yet you say, who touched me?'"*

We, also, should be amazed at how sensitive He is today to what we feel and aspire to in the secret depths of our hearts. We sometimes feel lost in the crowd before Him, and we are tempted to imagine that there are so many other pressing concerns claiming His attention that our problems and fears and hopes can never mean much to Him. But we deceive ourselves. We are often told in the New Testament that even though Jesus Christ is God, and is now exalted to the throne of the universe, He has not ceased to be still the same man, as sensitive to the touch of individual unexpressed human need as He was amongst this crowd in Galilee. Though He is the one mediator between God and all mankind, He remains for ever Himself "the man Christ Jesus" (i Tim. ii. 6). He has the whole world to care for, but He also cares for us. The fact that the burden of the life and destiny of all the mass of suffering humanity is before His eyes and is His responsibility, does not alter the fact that in the midst of it the most secret trembling inarticulate prayer of the solitary sufferer can gain His whole attention and loving concern.

But this woman made a very serious error in her attitude

to Jesus as she came up to Him in the crowd. She wanted only healing and strength from Him but not personal love. Instead of coming to Him as a person who would be interested to hear her case and consider her exact need and meet it with all His personal sympathy and care on the basis of a new and lasting friendship, she approached Him rather as if He were merely a centre of healing power into which she wanted to plug only for a moment. As we have already mentioned, her mind was full of superstitious ideas as she touched Him. Perhaps she had heard a current superstition that the corner of a religious teacher's robe could give off a special virtue if people held on to it. Her plan was to creep up behind Him to steal a little of His virtue without His suspecting it and then to disappear back into the crowd, without ever having had a personal face-to-face meeting with Him.

Jesus even responded to her superstitious faith. He healed her body as soon as she touched Him. But He corrected her superstition and forced on her the interview she had tried to avoid. *"He looked around to see who had done it."* He gave her no chance to escape the love that wanted to treat her as a personal friend and to save her heart and mind as well as her body. And when she found that she was really being sought out by such a love she gave Him the response of frankness and trust that He sought from her. *"The woman, knowing what had been done to her, came in fear and trembling and fell down before him and told him the whole truth."*

There are many of us today like this woman. We also want to enjoy the vague experiences or feelings or influence that, we believe, can somehow be caught from Jesus Christ if we mingle with the crowds around Him or go through certain ceremonies. Yet at the same time we seek to avoid the personal encounter with Him which He ultimately demands. We like being in the "atmosphere" of a big religious gathering because we feel it somehow does us good. We like the "something" that, we feel, hovers around an old Church building if we have the privilege of worshipping in it. We come to communion because we have a half-formed superstitious belief that the eating and drinking of the bread and wine almost automatically carries with it an ennobling and strengthening influence. We want baptism for our children because in a vague way we feel that it must do something there and then to the child. A great deal of superstition is often mingled with our Christian faith.

There may be, as in the case of this woman, a real and desperate faith mixed up with this superstition. Jesus did actually heal this woman at the moment she touched Him with her superstitious faith. And therefore we must acknowledge that He may be blessing many today whose religious observances are cluttered up with superstitions. He alone can discern the beginnings of the real faith that may be there already. But we must remember that Jesus in no way encouraged her superstition. He immediately arrested her and corrected her ideas. *"Daughter,"* He said to her, *"your faith has made you well; go in peace and be healed of your disease."* He made her see clearly that it was not because of her superstitious touch on His garment but only because of the Word that He sought to speak to her, in this face to face encounter with her answering faith, that He had healed her and given her true peace. Faith alone can ultimately save and heal us. And such faith can spring only from a living face to face encounter with the Jesus Christ who constantly speaks to us through His Word. Apart from such a relationship of personal trust in Him who speaks His trustworthy Word, there can be no true permanent peace nor healing for the sicknesses of mankind.

THE FEEDING OF THE
FIVE THOUSAND

The apostles returned to Jesus, and told him all that they had done and taught. And he said to them, "Come away by yourselves to a lonely place, and rest a while." For many were coming and going, and they had no leisure even to eat. And they went away in the boat to a lonely place by themselves. Now many saw them going, and knew them, and they ran there on foot from all the towns, and got there ahead of them. As he landed he saw a great throng, and he had compassion on them, because they were like sheep without a shepherd; and he began to teach them many things. And when it grew late, his disciples came to him and said, "This is a lonely place, and the hour is now late; send them away, to go into the country and villages round about and buy themselves something to eat." But he answered them, "You give them something to eat." And they said to him, "Shall we go and buy two hundred denarii worth of bread, and give it to them to eat?" And he said to them, "How many loaves have you? Go and see." And when they had found out, they said, "Five, and two fish." Then he commanded them all to sit down by companies upon the green grass. So they sat down in groups, by hundreds and by fifties. And taking the five loaves and the two fish he looked up to heaven, and blessed, and broke the loaves, and gave them to the disciples to set before the people; and he divided the two fish among them all. And they all ate and were satisfied. And they took up twelve baskets full of broken pieces and of the fish. And those who ate the loaves were five thousand men.

Mk. vi. 30–44.

Jesus was often unpopular. On many occasions He failed to hold the man in the street. There are many pictures of Him in the Gospels, especially during His later days, with the crowds either deserting Him or bitterly opposed to Him. In the same way, in the course of its history, the Church has often been unpopular too. It has sometimes been very much a minority concern.

But there were occasions on which Jesus achieved real popularity, and eager crowds followed Him to the point of embarrassing His disciples. They hung on His words and wanted more when He had finished speaking. It is therefore not surprising that the Church also at times in its history has had an occasional taste of the popularity which Jesus Christ Himself also experienced.

Today the attitude of the majority of men to Christ and His Church varies in different situations. There are places where to be a Christian means the bearing of a real cross of suffering in contempt and isolation. But there are also other lands where the Church enjoys great prestige amongst eager crowds of people. The testimony of many ministers for instance, in the new housing areas of our own land is that, where an approach is made to men and women in the name of the Gospel of Christ, the crowds will tend to gather with eagerness to be taught and led. Such popularity may be as superficial as Jesus's popularity was in His own day. It may be a danger and temptation to the Church. It certainly faces the Church with a real challenge, and in the midst of it, even more than in the midst of unpopularity, the Church needs guidance from Christ as to how to act and shape its policy.

This miracle of the feeding of the five thousand has a profound meaning for the Church, whatever its circumstances. But it has especial relevance when we think of the dangers and the challenge that face the Church in a land where there are still crowds of people ready to flock round it today when they believe that Jesus Christ is in the midst of it to speak to them, and to help and save them.

OUR RESPONSIBILITY FOR THOSE WHO FLOCK ROUND US

There were many in this multitude round Jesus who had not the right motives for seeking Him. Indeed for this very reason Jesus had tried to avoid at least a section of this crowd, and had spoken hard things calculated to turn away those who were not sincerely seeking the Kingdom of God. But in the end of the day the crowd was still there, five thousand of them, and they had very little food, and there were no shops near at hand. The popularity of Jesus had thus created a problem for Him and for His disciples. Where were they all to feed now? How were their concrete needs to be catered for in a practical way? What was to be done to help them on the lowest level of their human want?

The disciples obviously felt that this was no affair of theirs, and they tried to contract out of all responsibility for answering these questions. Indeed as time went on they became nervous and embarrassed at the thought of the nasty situation that might develop if Jesus did not dismiss this crowd soon. "*This is a lonely place, and the hour is late; send them away to go into the country and villages round about to buy themselves something to eat.*" They were not sure whether Jesus was going to be able to cope with the practical problem here raised by His own sheer popularity. Could He really manage these people and keep the situation in hand when they all began to waken up to realise what time it really was and how far they had been led on round this lake by Jesus? They knew, of course, that so far Jesus had dealt adequately with every situation, especially with the problems caused by His own unpopularity. But could He deal with the problems caused here by His very popularity? Should He not now quickly contract out, stop encouraging this crowd, call it a day before He became involved in their hungry demand for food, and send them away before the whole thing became too much for Him?

This same situation of embarrassment due to the popularity of Jesus does arise for the Church today. Think, for instance, of the situation that faces a Church like ours in Scotland. We are looked to as a national Church in the midst of a community which claims to be Christian. The extent to which it lives up to this claim is a matter on which opinions differ, nevertheless there is a willingness to give the Church and the name of Jesus Christ an official place within the nation's life. But this means also that people come round us in thousands as they came round Jesus in thousands, and they expect a good deal. Where a new housing area is being built, they expect the Church to be there, ready to supply a building in which youth organisations can be carried on, and public worship observed, and the community served in all kinds of ways that are not always directly connected with the Gospel of forgiveness and soul-salvation. For they know that the Church is the Church of Christ who said "Come to me all who labor and are heavy-laden and I will give you rest" (Mt. xi. 28) and that seems to them to be a very broad invitation implying a great deal. When a social problem arises in our country, men look to the Church and expect the Church to be in on the business of trying to solve it, not simply by talk but also by action. For they know that the Church is Christ's, who wept over the city when He thought of all its problems and sorrows and hardness of heart. Many of the young people of our land, even though uncommitted in mind and heart are ready to come round the Church for a bit, and to give it a chance to make something of them and say something vital to them, for they know that the Church is the Church of the Christ who became a growing youth for the sake of growing youth. Many little children throng some of our crowded Sunday Schools and juvenile organisations because their parents know that Christ said, "Let the children come to me, do not hinder them" (Mk. ix. 14). Couples come to have their weddings celebrated within the Church and they do so because in a vague way they connect Jesus with weddings and with home-building. The vague popularity of Jesus Christ today causes many parish ministers to become almost wearied and embarrassed by the numbers who come requesting His services for their homes, their sick, their children, their community life. Are we willing to accept our full responsibility for those who are thus drawn round us because we are Christ's and have Christ in our midst?

It is easy to avoid the difficulty and embarrassment simply by saying, "It is not the job of the Church to cater for the community around it in such a comprehensive way." We feel that we simply cannot cope to the full with the demands that a ministry of compassion and love will have to face at the heart of a needy multitude of people such as are around us. Therefore we are tempted to assert that the Church need care only to preach the Gospel of forgiveness and salvation and cater for the purely "spiritual" needs of the community, and having done thus it can with good conscience leave it to the government or secular organisations to set up community centres to which many of the thousands who now flock round Jesus Christ can turn to find many of the things they mistakenly expected Christ to provide. There are those who say that the Church should accept responsibility only for those about whom it is certain that they are the converted.

To take up this attitude is simply to echo the cry of the disciples in their embarrassment over this multitude of five thousand. *"Send them away."* Let the government cater for them from birth to the grave. Let the national health service be their comfort in life and in death. Let the local registrar marry them and, indeed, divorce and re-marry them as he wills. *"Send them away,"* and if the government fails, let each of them be responsible for his own material and social welfare! By this attitude and by these reasonings we try to contract out of the dangers and responsibilities in which Christ's popularity tends to involve us, in this modern world with its masses of people.

In face of our temptation to say *"Send them away,"* let us remember His word to the disciples in that critical situation in the desert. *"But he answered them, 'You give them something to eat'."* We must not try to contract out of our responsibility too easily. Christ's words and Christ's action in this wilderness imply that the Church has a responsibility not only for the committed who come round it, but also for the uncommitted multitude who have not yet made up their minds, and are merely interested. In any land where the Church is given freedom, or even a welcome, where Christ's teaching is circulated and acknowledged, there the Church has a tremendous responsibility for facing the needs of the whole community in His name. Certainly we must not be too afraid of disappointing or offending those who come round us. After all they may soon discover that our ability to produce for them the bread that perishes is very limited, and that we talk a great deal about the true bread that comes down from above. Nevertheless, Jesus's first word to His disciples was one that forced them to try to cater on an ordinary level for the multitude which His popularity had gathered round them.

Our Resources are adequate for the Task

Jesus in this miracle gave a unique and wonderful sign that His resources are completely adequate to cater for the needs of all who are drawn towards Him through His mission in this world. *"They need not go away"* (Mt. XIV. 16), He said *"You give them something to eat."*

"They need not go away!" When Jesus Christ is in our midst we will have the resources to deal adequately with the human situation that His popularity may create. We need not be

nervous as to whether we can "hold the people" and deal with the practical problems that arise. He himself in our midst will always be adequate to meet the growing demands of His own work and mission on every level. If His words and compassion and influence draw a multitude, He will cater for the multitude.

He not only promised this in His words to the disciples, but He performed the sign to show that His word was true. He fed the multitude there and then, and by the miracle He again is repeating: "With Me in the midst, My disciples in every age will have adequate resources to meet the demands of My work."

This miracle must often have comforted the disciples as the Church spread, and men and women flocked round them, and the problems grew. How were they going to manage? They would think back, and remember the miracles of His feeding of the crowds. In face of these how could they fail to understand that Jesus Christ in the midst of the Church is always adequate for the emergency or crisis in the affairs of His people? His Church will have bread enough and to spare. He is never baffled or at a loss in the midst of the ticklish human situations that arise in Christian work. He always knows what He will do.

It is important for us to seal all this on our minds, for it is often our nervousness and unbelief about Jesus's adequacy for His work today, that prevents us from going ahead with bolder plans for mission. If we were moved more by our compassion and love for men we would make larger plans for bringing to all men the bread of life that alone can satisfy their hunger of heart. But our plans are often dictated not by the breadth of Christ's love but rather by the smallness of our faith. We forget His adequacy to meet whatever situation His own love will bring about within the Church, and we plan, almost unconsciously, to avoid the awkward situation that might require great faith in Jesus. But this story assures us that Christ's resources are endless. When men of the world set out on an enterprise they calculate that they have just so much energy and capital to expend. They plan, knowing that after they have spent so much there will come a point when they will have less and less to put out in expenditure. But with Christ it is different. What He can give at the end is better and more adequate than what He supplies at the beginning of an enterprise, for at the end of this miracle there were left "*twelve baskets full of broken pieces, and of the fish.*"

We ourselves come into all this a good deal, for He worked this miracle of proving His adequacy through the agency of His own disciples. This is quite a remarkable development in His work, for in so many other miracles He had used simply His own direct agency. But He says here, "*You* give them something to eat." They themselves were most inadequate, for they were trembling half-believing men. But He used them in spite of their unbelief. They had little to offer. The most they could collect was five loaves and two fish, but what were those among so many? Yet He took what they brought and gave thanks and used it and used them.

But the glorious adequacy of our inadequate resources only appears if we surrender them into His hands to use both them and us in an offering of obedience and faith. What matters is not so much the greatness of the gifts as the completeness of the surrender. If the task is His will, let us prove Him by setting out to do it, and as we go ahead in faith, the promise of this miracle is simply that He will do it with us and will complete it in glorious adequacy. "Bring the full tithes into the storehouse, that there may be food in my house; and thereby put me to the test, says the Lord of hosts, if I will not open the windows of heaven for you, and pour down for you an overflowing blessing" (Mal. III. 10).

Again, let us remember that this miracle has more than a "spiritual" significance. Certainly, as we shall see, what happened in this feeding of the multitude is a sign of a deep spiritual mystery. But it was accomplished through giving loaves and fishes to people who were really hungry. For most men today it is not loaves and fishes that are the important things, it is rather money. Perhaps here is the root of much of our failure. Jesus Christ today could work even greater spiritual miracles than this one amongst the multitudes if the people of the Church would put more of their money at His disposal. But we will not give Him even the small portion He looks for in order to make a start with us.

But Christ remains adequate in spite of our failures and weakness. He is able in every age to give through His disciples that which men around the Church really need, and in every age He will prove it. Yet this miracle is not necessarily a promise of ultimate success. Christ fed the five thousand adequately that day, but we are not told that He was so successful in bringing them all into the Kingdom of God. The evidences indeed, are that many of them deserted Him at the last. Yet in the midst of the failure He proved Himself adequate.

The Earthly and the Heavenly Bread

In the New Testament this miracle is told in such a way as to remind us of the perpetual miracle which Christ accomplishes in the midst of the Church. At the heart of the Church in every generation there takes place a mystery which constantly keeps the Church alive and renews the faith and vigour of its members. This is the miracle, that the risen exalted Christ continually enables the Church to partake of His own heavenly life and of the life of His resurrection Kingdom. This is the wonderful truth proclaimed every time the Church gathers at the Lord's table, and the bread, which is the symbol of His body and its heavenly life is handed out to men and eaten. All this is a sign that the Kingdom of Heaven has broken into the life of this world. That the glorious Messiah has come and in the wilderness of this world is now feeding His people with the first fruits of the life of the new Messianic age. He is giving them a foretaste of the glory of the world-to-come. All this was in Jesus's mind on the day when He used His disciples to feed the five thousand, and afterwards said, "I am the bread of life; he who comes to me shall not hunger, and he who believes in me shall never thirst. . . . Your fathers ate the manna in the wilderness and they died. This is the bread which comes down from heaven, that a man may eat of it and not die" (Jn. vi. 35, 49–50).

Certainly Jesus meant those who could think only on a material level to take to heart the very mundane lessons we have already taken from this miracle of His feeding of the multitudes. But many of the Jews expected their Messiah to come, and one of the signs of His presence was to be a banquet which He would hold with the true Israel of God. Jesus meant those who could understand to grasp from His action the truth that He was indeed the true Messiah of Israel, and to realise that already in receiving this bread from Him, they were members of the new and true Israel of which He was the Head and the King, and that the bread He was giving them was a sure pledge of the heavenly bread with which He would feed His people in the great Messianic banquet that would take place when the end of this world has finally ushered in the age-to-come in its full glory.

This miracle, and the words Christ uttered as He enacted it, is one of the guarantees we have from Him that as we gather at the Lord's table and take the bread and wine, He Himself is in the midst, the risen Messiah, to feed His Church, through the simple action we perform in faith, with the bread from heaven which is Himself, and which none but He can give. Because He is thus present in the midst, He makes our action of breaking, giving, taking and eating a truly glorious Messianic feast, strengthening us to continue our pilgrimage in this world and encouraging us to lift up our eyes with greater hope and expectation towards the world that is to come.

Moreover this miracle is also our guarantee that as we seek within the Church to feed one another with the bread of life which is His Word, He also will not fail to take our frail words spoken in His name, and perhaps poorly spoken, and use them as He used the offering of loaves and fishes that they brought Him that day in the wilderness, to satisfy the hungry multitudes who are looking to Him for the bread of life. How inadequate are the words we speak in the name of Jesus in our sermons and in our poor efforts at teaching in Sunday School and Bible Class! It is as stupid to think they can do Christ's work, as it was to think that these few loaves and fishes were enough for the thousands. And yet the constant miracle takes place every Sunday as we offer our words to Him for His service. Christ takes them, blesses them, gives them afresh to us, and as they are received, men receive the mystery of the life of the Word of God incarnate. Through the words which represent the flesh and blood of Jesus Christ they indeed eat the flesh of the Son of man, and drink His blood, and have eternal life. This miracle of the feeding of the five thousand is surely there in the New Testament to remind every preacher of the Word of God of the mystery that accompanies the proclamation of the Word.

ORDERLINESS AND CARE

There is a further lesson we can take from this miracle. The story gives an impression of the orderliness that must have been observed by Jesus and His disciples in the distribution of the bread. He made them all sit down in regular groups, and after a deliberate giving of thanks He gave to the disciples and the disciples to the multitude. Here where we are dealing with a deep spiritual mystery everything must be done "decently and in order" (1 Cor. xiv. 40). It is not unspiritual to attend carefully to the details of Church organisation, to the details of Church liturgy or to be concerned that ministers of the Gospel should be distributed in a sensible way in a country in parishes that are neither too small nor too large. To see to all this question of orderliness is part of our stewardship of the mystery of Christ and is linked up with His own self-giving to men.

Moreover, the care taken by Jesus and the disciples in collecting and preserving whatever was left over from the miracle is also remarkable. The twelve baskets that remained remind us that the provision of Christ for His work is certainly prodigal and overflowing. But the care taken over them reminds us that in dealing with the grace of God there can be no carelessness or presumption. Nothing is more free or more plentiful than Christ's bounty. Men can take what they need and He is ready to give more. But what He gives in His wealth, He can give only because for our sakes He became poor, and the bread of life is His body which was given for the life of the world.

THE WALKING ON THE SEA

Immediately he made his disciples get into the boat and go before him to the other side, to Bethsaida, while he dismissed the crowd. And after he had taken leave of them, he went into the hills to pray. And when evening came, the boat was out on the sea, and he was alone on the land. And he saw that they were distressed in rowing, for the wind was against them. And about the fourth watch of the night he came to them, walking on the sea. He meant to pass by them, but when they saw him walking on the sea they thought it was a ghost, and cried out; for they all saw him, and were terrified. But immediately he spoke to them and said, "Take heart, it is I; have no fear." And he got into the boat with them and the wind ceased. And they were utterly astounded, for they did not understand about the loaves, but their hearts were hardened.

Mk. vi. 45–52.

The Church on its way

"Immediately he made his disciples get into the boat and go before him to the other side." Jesus Himself planned this journey for His disciples. By themselves they would not have chosen to set out on that night, and very soon after starting they must have wondered why Jesus had insisted on their embarking without Him. It all had seemed rather a purposeless venture. They had been involved from the start in a very difficult struggle against wind and current, and now they were being forced to toil away with all their strength only to find themselves getting nowhere. They became depressed over their failure and weakness, and they found it hard not to be anxious as to whether in the end they were going to win through to the other side. They wondered why Jesus had led them into this. Certainly on a previous occasion when the storm had been far worse, He had stilled it by His Word when they awoke Him. But that had been during the day-time, and they had had His presence beside them in the boat. Now they were in darkness, and He was not with them, and the waves were indeed beginning to threaten. Why had He compelled them to come out into this depressing and difficult situation?

This has very often been Jesus's way with His Church. The

journey He made the disciples take that night is the kind of journey He has very often forced His Church to take in the course of its history. And the situation in which the disciples found themselves, is the kind of situation in which Jesus has often involved His Church throughout its earthly career. Indeed there have been many occasions in history when the Church has looked for a picture of itself in the New Testament and the nearest it could find was the picture of the disciples in this little boat, struggling desperately against the darkness and the waves, threatened for its life and not seeming to get anywhere! Often, when the Church has looked at itself frankly, tried honestly to sum up its real position, calculated its chances of progress or even survival against the huge forces that were trying to bar its advance and threaten its life, this picture of the little depressed boatload in the Gospel story has seemed the one that best fitted the real situation.

Does it fit us today—this picture of the Church in the world? We still have in our hymn books the verse, "Like a mighty army moves the Church of God," but in some countries of the world the Church has lost the initiative and is engaged in a desperate and apparently fatal struggle to save its life against overwhelming odds. In some parts it seems to be entirely losing the battle for the young in face of the attacks of a communism that can show more evidence of success and fresh vigour than the Church has given for generations. Even in a country like our own, the cold statistical figures of the number of the faithful within the Church do not make an impressive show when they are compared with figures of our population, and it can easily be argued that the Church is simply a minority body enjoying an undeserved prominence only because it can cling to certain privileges that some day soon may be taken away from it. And there are certainly not a few ministers of the Gospel who would admit that their task at times appears to be like that of the oarsmen in the boat on the Lake—a hard row against wind and tide with no visible progress made, and a tendency to depression settling down amongst the crew.

THE ONE AND ONLY DANGER

But the story of what happened shows us that there was only one real danger facing the disciples that night. The real danger lay not in the power of the wind and the waves, not in any evil forces lurking in the darkness, but in the hardness that settled down in their own unbelieving hearts.

"*Their hearts were hardened*" is the comment St. Mark makes as he tells us of their behaviour during this incident. This was the reason why they had become so depressed and terrified.

This hardness of heart had a strange effect on them. It prevented them from appreciating in any way the care and the help that Christ was giving them all through that journey and especially at the last moment of crisis. They left Him "*alone on the land,*" the story says, and they thought that His parting gesture meant that He was committing them to the mercies of the waves and the darkness and had other things to attend to. But Mark insists that all the time they were indulging in their gloomy and distressing questionings and inward murmurings, Jesus Himself never ceased to have them on His mind. "*He went into the hills to pray*" we are told here. And all through that time of prayer He watched them in their trouble. "*He saw that they were distressed in rowing, for the wind was against them.*" What else could He do in His prayer, but pray for them? Yet all the while they felt forsaken by Him and finally when He did come near to help them, the same hardness of their hearts made them interpret the very signs of His presence as an evil portent. "*They thought it was a ghost, and cried out; for they all saw him and were terrified.*" All this stupidity because "*their hearts were hardened.*"

This is our chief danger within the Church today. The New Testament assures us in countless promises that Christ is watching over His Church today with the utmost care in every detail for its true welfare. He never ceases to pray for it to His Father. He seeks constantly to feed, encourage, cleanse and renew it, and for this purpose He constantly comes into our midst to speak His Word and to make His sacraments effective. But because our hearts become "*hardened*" by unbelief in the midst of all the difficulties and temptations that surround us, we forget all this. We reckon ourselves forsaken by Christ, and become quite blind to His love and care for us, and unable to tell when He is near.

This "hardening of the heart" is spoken of in the Bible as

something very sinister. It was this hardness of heart in Pharaoh that made him try to thwart God's purposes to let the Children of Israel go free, and finally led to his own destruction (Exod. VII. 13; VIII. 32, IX. 7). It was this hardness of heart in the Children of Israel that made them reject the Word of God and His prophets (Is. VI. 10), and finally the Messiah Himself when He came (Rom. XI. 25). It was the manifestation of this hardening of the heart in the Pharisees that grieved Jesus greatly (Mk. III. 5) during His earthly life and finally led men to crucify Him.

Here, then, in this story we are being given an urgent warning about ourselves. It is possible that those who are Jesus's disciples can become, temporarily at any rate, motivated by a spirit and attitude that has fearful implications. The disease that made God's worst enemies His enemies indeed, that gripped the hearts of those who always thwarted Him in His purposes and finally crucified His son—this disease lurks in our hearts too, and can grip us very easily and very quickly, unless we *"understand"* and are watchful.

It is because of this hardening of our hearts that we too behave as the disciples behaved on the lake that night. As they grew weary, and depressed and disheartened and their strength was sapped, so do we. As they felt forsaken by Christ so do we. As they dismissed the very idea of His help from their minds, so do we. Simply because our hearts become hardened! And in this mood we can be led to do very stupid things. It is a mood that can lead Churches and Church courts to gloomy policies of fear and defeatism that result in retreat on the Church's frontiers, and a timid apologetic approach where there is an attempt to advance. It is a mood that can lead congregations to resort to panic methods and unworthy ways of raising money for their work, since it involves a complete lack of faith in the active care of Christ Himself for these matters. All the time, as in this story, He is living for us, praying for us, watching, caring, ready to intervene. All the time we have promises that proclaim this to us if we will listen to them even for a moment. But we allow ourselves and our situation to be ruled by the fear, depression, unbelief and cynicism that well up from the hardness of our hearts.

To Jesus Himself there was no other danger to the Church

or to the Christian so serious as the danger that comes from this hardening. Jesus by this time had already proved to His disciples that He was Lord over the waves, over disease, over the devils, over death, and that they need fear no evil and no want. As we read the Gospels we see that up to this point He had been able to solve every problem that had faced Him, except this one problem—the inward state of their hearts that prevented them from understanding that He was indeed Lord. But His coming to them that night *"in the fourth watch of the night"* was another attempt on His part to save them from this one and only danger to their souls.

THE LORD WHO COMES

But it was not till *"about the fourth watch of the night"* that He came to them. That was very late indeed. They had a long period of trial and a long period of failure to undergo before He came. Might He not have come sooner? But it was sometimes His custom to delay like this. He is so much in control of the situation that He can afford to wait until it almost seems to be out of hand. He can let our failures run their course and then come and sort things out for a better ending than constant success could ever have given us. He can, as in the case of Lazarus, delay his action and allow death to have five days' start before He shows how God can be glorified through His very delay. But He knows what is the best time to intervene far better than we do, and if He seems to us to delay for a small moment too long for us to bear, it will always prove to have been good for us. "For a brief moment I forsook you, but with great compassion will I gather you. In overflowing wrath for a moment I hid my face from you, but with everlasting love I will have compassion on you, says the Lord, your Redeemer" (Is. LIV. 7–8). Sometimes He delays in order to let us understand how futile and unsuccessful all our hard efforts can be when in the hardness of heart we forget to look to Him.

Yet we need not fear. The time of His coming is often the very moment when we seem to be at the end of our powers and our patience, when the waves of danger or persecution mount high and the opposing winds are at their fiercest and the darkness is most perplexing. Then He will Himself not fail to come and reveal Himself as the Lord who has such control over the waves that He can tread them with His feet and control them as He wills. "*He came to them walking on the sea.*"

The word He spoke to them when He came was the same word as God spoke to Moses at the burning bush when He told him His name (Ex. III. 14). "*It is I,*" or, "I am." He was trying to recall to their minds the story of Moses and the Exodus from Egypt, the story of how the Lord God proved Himself master of the waves, and was able to make them do His will. He was trying also to remind them of the words of psalmists and prophets about God's Lordship over the sea. "Thou didst trample the sea with thy horses, the surging of the mighty waters" (Hab. III. 15). "Thy way was through the sea, thy path through the great waters; yet thy footprints were unseen" (Ps. LXXVII. 19). Here He is. He is none other than the Lord who does these things and about whom these things are said! "*Take heart, it is I, have no fear.*"

But even when He was there, it was only when the disciples recognised His voice that they knew it was His own presence, and their fear of the elements vanished. They recognised Him not through His visible shape or action, not through the figure they could see dimly with their eyes moving amongst the spray and the mist, but through the tone of His voice as He spoke to them His word of assurance and victory. What they saw with their eyes brought only terror to their hearts for when they looked "*they thought it was a ghost and cried out; for they all saw him, and were terrified.*" But what they heard with their ears was the voice of the true shepherd and master, and there could be no mistaking any other voice for this.

That is why we must learn to listen with our ears more than to look with our eyes if we want to be assured of the presence of Christ in our midst. In the Easter appearances of our Lord to His disciples it is noticeable that at first they did not recognise Him, yet recognition came after He started to speak to them (Jn. XX. 16, XXI. 5–7; Lk. XXIV. 32). His promise is "my sheep hear my voice, and I know them, and they follow me" (Jn. X. 27). This is why in the Church we must listen constantly to the preaching of the Word of God, for it is by speaking through the Holy Scriptures that Christ makes His presence known to us in the midst of our troubles and causes us to hear His voice. Christianity will always be a faith in which the ears will play a larger part than the eyes. Moreover, we would do well to take to heart the warning here against what is ghostlike and vague in its shape. When Christ comes to reveal Himself and convey His power to us He seeks to do so through speaking a clear and definite Word. We require to become more suspicious than we have been of the vague spiritual influences and uplifting indefinable feelings that are sometimes offered to us in His name, in place of the clear proclamation of His glory and majesty and love, of His definite promises and commands, as these are set forth for us in the Bible. The cult of personality, of the "numinous," or of the emotionally exciting, will never suffice to cure us of our fear and listlessness and lack of faith. Nothing but the Word of Christ can register in any way behind the hardness of heart that prevents us from really seeing or believing or understanding or succeeding. The Word alone is the sword that can penetrate through to our real heart and conscience and bring hope and assurance and new zeal to the Church in its sorry plight.

That night on the lake Jesus spoke such a Word. And in succeeding years when the disciples preached the Gospel they often told this story as an example of the miracle that can happen when Christ comes into the midst in the darkness and depression and storm to speak His Word to His voyaging Church.

His Word proves Him indeed to be Lord over the waves and winds, over all the forces of evil and darkness and destruction that may be ranged against us. As He spoke it, He stood on the waves to prove how little their apparent fierceness and force could prevail over Him. It is the Word of the risen Lord. There is nothing through which He cannot or will not come in order to speak this Word and to save His Church. When we hear it we know He walks with us as the serene conqueror over sin, the world, the devil and death—over everything that has made us afraid. It is the Word that says to us, "In the world you have tribulation, but be of good cheer, I have overcome the world" (Jn. xvi. 33). His coming in this way ensures that the Church will fulfil the mission on which He has sent it. John finishes his account of this incident by saying: "Then they were glad to take Him into the boat, and immediately the boat was at the land to which they were going" (Jn. vi. 21).

Here, then, is the wonderful mystery in the faith of which the

Church must ever live and hope. Jesus will always come into our midst in His own good time, to revive, to encourage, to strengthen His people in the battle, the toiling, the task, to give them vision and assurance and ultimately to lead them through the darkness and the great waters.

And this is not all. He who died for His Church upon the Cross ever lives for us at the right hand of Almighty God. This also means unfailing power and certain victory for us in our battle and our task.

When Moses was leading the Old Testament Church through the wilderness, the Amalekites came and fought against it. The children of Israel had few weapons and no military training. But Moses, Aaron and Hur went up to the mountain top. And "whenever Moses held up his hand, Israel prevailed; and whenever he lowered his hand, Amalek prevailed" (Exod. XVII. 11). When we read this New Testament story again, and see Christ looking down from the mountain-side on His little boatload of distressed disciples in their sad plight, and lifting up His hands on their behalf, we are reminded of how even the prayers of Moses on the desert mountain prevailed for the safety and victory of Israel. But all this is a mere foreshadowing of the victory that the intercession of the exalted Christ for ever at the right hand of God is bound for ever to win for all His people.

THE SYROPHOENICIAN WOMAN

And Jesus went away from there and withdrew to the district of Tyre and Sidon. And behold, a Canaanite woman from that region came out and cried, "Have mercy on me, O Lord, Son of David; my daughter is severely possessed by a demon." But he did not answer her a word. And his disciples came and begged him, saying, "Send her away, for she is crying after us." He answered, "I was sent only to the lost sheep of the house of Israel." But she came and knelt before him, saying, "Lord, help me." And he answered, "It is not fair to take the children's bread and throw it to the dogs." She said, "Yes, Lord, yet even the dogs eat the crumbs that fall from their master's table." Then Jesus answered her, "O woman, great is your faith! Be it done f r you **as** you desire." And her daughter was healed instantly.

Mt. xv. 21–28.

FAITH SEES BEHIND THE EVILS OF LIFE

This woman refused to accept the tragic circumstances of her life as inevitable. Her daughter was seized by an illness that was distressing and terrible in its symptoms. What was she to do? What attitude was she to take? No doubt she at first went to the doctors. They gave her some hope that a cure was possible and encouraged her to take heart. But when they saw that after their best efforts there was no sign of improvement they naturally emphasised the hopeless nature of the case and indicated that there was no power on earth that could cure this little girl. She also went to her neighbours for comfort and strength. They too encouraged her at the start to believe that it was not so bad as appeared. But as the weary months passed and they saw that the child's condition was obviously deteriorating they felt it was a pity that she was not facing up to reality, and they gradually began to advise her not to fret so much and to resign herself bravely to the will of Heaven and to her own and her daughter's fate.

But the woman refused to accept and bear it with a resigned spirit. She refused to submit, or to admit into her mind the slightest suggestion that what had happened to her little girl was the will of God. "Seems more like the Devil's work to me,"

she said to herself, "that my child should be lying there de-
mented and distressed." It was the will of the Devil and not of
God, she decided. God's will was that her child should be cured.
She resolved that she could never accept this triumph of evil,
and would give herself no rest till God's will was done.

What lay behind her taking such an outlook? It is possible
that she knew something of the teaching about God in the Old
Testament, for she later used the language of the Old Testament when she asked Jesus to heal her daughter. Many parts
of these Scriptures inspire hope where the circumstances of life
are despairing, and they certainly reveal a God who seeks to
banish evil things. They may have inspired this woman. She
must also have at some time heard that Jesus was going about
and healing cases like that of the child. Reports reached her
that He was a kind and merciful man, this Jesus. Certainly she
knew there might be difficulties, for He was a Jew and she
was a Canaanite—a heathen in His eyes. Would He receive
such as her, and help her? But she heard that He gave invitations to people to come to Him. "Come to me," He had said, "all
who labour and are heavy laden, and I will give you rest"
(Mt. xi. 28), and "him who comes to me, I will not cast out"
(Jn. vi. 37). She had heard things like that about Him, and
that He had never yet turned anyone away. There He was,
inviting people in trouble. Here was her girl lying under the
power of Satan. She would go and make sure that nothing was
left undone in the way of bringing Jesus's help to her home.
*"And Jesus . . . withdrew to the district of Tyre and Sidon. And
behold a Canaanite woman from that region came out and cried, 'Have
mercy on me, O Lord, Son of David; my daughter is severely possessed
by a demon'."*

The faith of many of us is lacking in this respect. We submit
too meekly to the disorders and hindrances that prevent God's
will being done around us. We resign ourselves too quickly to
the failures that are due to causes that are sinful and often
sinister. We are far too ready to raise the pious sigh, "Thy will
be done," in the midst of circumstances that are nothing short
of a satanic denial of the will of God. We have the idea that
such infinite resignation is the characteristic and climax of
great faith. But in nine cases out of ten, faith should see in the
evils of life, not God's will but the Devil's will and should seek

restlessly and desperately to have these evils removed by the power of Jesus Christ.

Certainly there are the other cases where God asks us to bear as His will things that are obviously of evil design and accomplishment. Paul was faced with something in his circumstances that he found so hard to bear he called it a "a thorn in the flesh." He tells us that he looked on it as being satanic in its origin, and he prayed much to God to remove it from his life. But ultimately God told him to cease resistance and to accept it (1 Cor. XII. 7–10). Our Lord Himself saw His cross as such an evil and abhorrent thing that He prayed in agony to be spared its bitterness. "My Father if it be possible, let this cup pass from me." But He ultimately resigned Himself to it because it was God's will. "Nevertheless, not as I will, but as thou wilt" (Mt. XXVI. 39).

Therefore for us too faith can mean resignation to what seems in itself something very evil. But at the same time, if our faith is true and living, we will always see evil as evil as it truly is, even when we must be resigned. We will, however, more often see in the evils of life a challenge not to relax and resign but to rebel. Few of us, for instance, even in the direst crisis, will be able to resign ourselves readily to the use of nuclear bombs as God's will for our nation. Over a century ago most of our Protestant Churches resigned themselves to the heathenism of the non-Christian world. And when young William Carey proposed to a group of ministers that they should plan to send missionaries abroad, he was told, "Sit down, young man. When God wills to convert the heathen He will do it without you." They saw heathenism as something to be accepted as if it were the will of God. Carey saw it as something to be rebelled against as if it were the will of the Devil. Many apparently tragic and sinister things may have to be accepted as God's will, but it should not be accepted as God's will that people in this world should suffer and die from diseases for which He has put a cure in the hands of the medical profession. It is not to be accepted as God's will that there should be filthy and dismal slum conditions in a land where there are the resources to provide better homes. It is not to be accepted as God's will that the world should be so darkened by lack of knowledge of the Gospel, when He has shined into this world the light of the glory of Jesus Christ. It is not to be accepted as God's will that we who profess the Christian faith should have gloom, consistent moral defeat, and tragic defect of character as our lot, when Jesus Christ has promised us so much in the way of gladness and confidence and victory. In a book on this subject written more than a generation ago with the title, *The Faith that Rebels*, D. S. Cairn points out that if we study the references to faith in the teaching of Jesus, "the faith to which they call us is to anything rather than acquiescence, it is rather to uncompromising rebellion against what seems the natural course of events. Men are encouraged to seek deliverance from diseases incurable by the medical science of their day, from maladies that by long neglect have become chronic, from premature death, and even from the untamed forces of nature itself. What are we moderns to make of such an astonishing saying as this: 'Have faith in God, for verily I say unto you that if ye have faith as a grain of mustard seed, ye shall say to this mountain, "Be thou removed hence, and it shall obey you?"' "

Faith sees behind Appearance in Jesus

It is obvious that when this woman came to Jesus with her request, He was thrilled. He rejoiced when people sought to co-operate with Him in His mission to destroy the works of the Devil (i Jn. iii. 8). His later appraisal of her, "O woman, great is your faith," was a cry of genuine admiration, and He saw it from the start.

But He greeted her in a manner that was, for Him, quite strange and unusual. For a long time He acted towards her as if He was completely indifferent to her plight. He threw up difficulty after difficulty in her way. He, as it were, put on a mask, another face than His true face. Perhaps He was testing her faith, knowing that if it was genuine it would see through to His heart and would never be put off by His outward behaviour. Perhaps He wanted to show the disciples the greatness of her faith shining out in all its true qualities as she persisted and argued with Him and beat Him down.

At first He was deliberately silent. "*He did not answer her a word.*" It must have been a sustained period of silence, for, during it, her cries to Him became so loud and monotonously persistent that the disciples were unable to stand the strain and embarrassment, and they pled with Jesus that if He had no intention of doing anything for her He would at least tell her definitely, and end the agony and suspense. "*And his disciples came and begged him, saying, 'Send her away, for she is crying after us'.*"

But the next stage was almost as agonising as the silence. He plagued her mind with a baffling suggestion. Perhaps she was not one of the elect. "*I was sent only to the lost sheep of the house of Israel.*" It was another rebuff, given in a very gentle way. If Jesus had said this with any air of finality, it would have meant the end of all hope for her. But He could not have done so. It was true, certainly, but it was only half-true, and He must have indicated in some way by His manner of speech that perhaps the closed door might yet open.

Therefore she took encouragement, even from His rebuff, and with increased boldness "*she came and knelt before him, saying, 'Lord, help me'.*" And once she was there, she had no more real difficulty. Jesus likened her, as a heathen woman bursting into His circle of Jewish disciples and interrupting His teaching, to a little dog yelping at a father who was trying to feed his hungry children with little food. "*It is not fair,*" He said, "*to take the children's bread and throw it to the dogs.*" But in a flash she saw that even this rebuke meant that He was really seriously thinking over what it would mean to help her, and she seized on His very words and twisted them round and extracted every particle of hope that she could get out of them and threw them back at Him triumphantly. "*Yes Lord,*" she replied, "*yet even the dogs eat the crumbs that fall from their master's table.*" "Was this not a master stroke," comments Luther here. "She snares Christ in His own words."

If this woman had taken Jesus at His face value, she would have been put off completely, and her daughter might never have been cured. But faith never takes God at His face value. Faith, under such circumstances, never believes that God is as He appears to be. This woman, then, refused to take Jesus at His face value. She believed the word that she had heard about Him, in spite of His appearance. She believed the Word that He Himself had spoken. "Come to me, all who labor and are heavy laden, and I will give you rest" (Mt. xi. 28). Therefore she took Jesus's silence as a challenge to become more and more persistent in her requests and prayers. She took His rebukes as a challenge to take up the battle with Him and argue with Him on the basis of His own words. She was emboldened by His whole attitude to assert her will against His apparent indifference and to win Him over.

Sometimes God appears to treat us as Jesus treated this Syrophoenician. We too become plagued and troubled by His silence in answer to our prayers, and by the rebukes we seem to hear at the heart of His silence. There are times when, for us, neither Church-going, nor Bible reading, nor prayers, nor enthusiastic effort, can seem to bring about any break in the silence that prevails between Heaven and ourselves. A friend of Thomas Erskine, a great Scottish Churchman, tells how he once spoke of "the awful silence of God and how it becomes oppressive and the heart longed to hear some audible voice in answer to its cry." Then he quoted from the verse from the Psalms: "To Thee, O Lord, I call; my rock, be not deaf to me, lest, if thou be silent to me, I become like those who go down to the Pit" (Ps. xxviii. 1).

Moreover at the same time we may find ourselves troubled by the apparent rebukes that God is administering to us. Things may happen to us that we can interpret as the consequences of our own folly and sin, and the fact that God allows such things to come upon us depresses us and makes us tempted to feel that He is indeed against us.

When it happens like that with us, we must not allow ourselves to be brought down into the pit of despair. We must believe, not in the silence of God but in the Word of God. The silence of God is only an appearance, the Word of God expresses His true nature. We must see in the silence of God nothing else but a challenge to ourselves to persist in our praying till we have some response to our knocking at the door of Heaven. Is not His Word, "Knock and it will be opened to you?" (Lk. xi. 9). "For if when in a house," says Luther again, "He hides Himself in a chamber and will not that the entrance be opened to any, nevertheless do not give way, but follow. Beat the doors of the chamber and clamour. For the very highest sacrifice is never to cease from praying and seeking until we conquer Him."

Moreover if God is rebuking us we must realise that it is precisely because He loves us and wants us that He is doing so.

"For the Lord disciplines him whom He loves, and chastises every son whom He receives" (Heb. XII. 6). We must listen to what He is saying in His rebukes. But we must remember that in rebuking us He is indeed speaking to us and dealing with us, and He wants an answer back from us, in the same way as Jesus wanted an answer back from this woman. A great commentator on this miracle again quotes Luther here. "Like her, thou must give God right in all He says against thee, and yet must not stand off from praying, till thou overcomest as she overcame, till thou hast turned the very charges made against thee into arguments and proofs of thy need, till thou too hast taken Christ in His own words." And he adds his own comment that we are to learn here, "to wring a Yea from God's Nay," or rather "to hear the deep-hidden Yea which many times lurks under His seeming Nay."

"Faith sees far into the heart of God," said Joseph Parker. The heart of God is expressed in His Word. "Come to me, all who labor and are heavy laden, and I will give you rest." That is His true attitude towards His people, and nothing can alter it. The faith that lays hold of this Word can endure long periods of silence, it can persist in the face of the most terrible rebukes, because it rests not on earthly appearances, or on changing moods and feelings, but on the Word of God which endures for ever.

FAITH OVERCOMES IN THE END

"Then Jesus answered her, 'O woman, great is your faith. Be it done for you as you desire.' And her daughter was healed instantly."

Here is the end of this battle of wills and wits in which this woman has joined with Jesus. *"As you desire."* She has overcome. Because of her faith and persistence in laying hold of His love in such a determined manner, He gives way and yields to her importunity, to her clever wrestling with His words, to her desperate prayer. "He who showed at first as though He would have denied her the smallest boon, now opens to her the full treasure house of His grace, and bids her to help herself, to carry away what she will."

Was Jesus here not teaching His disciples as well as healing this woman's child? They are to learn that God will yield to the prayer of faith and to the will behind the prayer of faith.

Faith laying hold of the love of God will be able to draw from the heart of God a response that would not otherwise be given. God's will is flexible, as flexible as His love, where it encounters human need and human importunity in prayer. God can indeed be laid hold of, and argued with, and constrained by desperate human faith in a real battle in which He allows Himself to be overcome by faith. The secret of prayer was perhaps never more succinctly put than by Luther when he said, "The word, Father, hath overcome God."

Yet God will yield, not to the proud self-seeking human will that is not reconciled to Himself by faith, but rather to the will such as this woman had. He yields to the will that is inspired by His own love, and His own passion that men might be saved, to the will that is inspired by a hatred of evil and a burning desire to see Christ's Kingdom come. Prayer is overcoming God by His own love and by His own Spirit who inspires all our rebellious prayers.

Of course we will have to resign ourselves to waiting a long time for an answer. With such rebellion in our hearts we may have to resign ourselves to many an evil, to many a death, to many an ailment and infirmity and failure. But even in resigning ourselves we do not admit that these things are the last word. The last word is God's Word and God's victory. That means the abolition of all death, disease, pain and the Devil's rule. And some manifest share in that victory can indeed be ours already, because we have the Victor with us, all the day, even into the end of the world.

THE DEAF MAN AT DECAPOLIS AND
THE BLIND MAN AT BETHSAIDA

Then he returned from the region of Tyre, and went through Sidon to the Sea of Galilee, through the region of the Decapolis. And they brought to him a man who was deaf and had an impediment in his speech; and they besought him to lay his hand upon him. And taking him aside from the multitude privately, he put his fingers into his ears, and he spat and touched his tongue; and looking up to heaven, he sighed, and said to him, "Ephphatha," that is, "Be opened." And his ears were opened, his tongue was released, and he spoke plainly. And he charged them to tell no one; but the more he charged them, the more zealously they proclaimed it. And they were astonished beyond measure, saying, "He has done all things well; he even makes the deaf hear and the dumb speak."

Mk. vii. 31–37.

And they came to Bethsaida. And some people brought to him a blind man, and begged him to touch him. And he took the blind man by the hand, and led him out of the village; and when he had spit on his eyes and laid his hands upon him, he asked him, "Do you see anything?" And he looked up and said, "I see men; but they look like trees, walking." Then again he laid his hands upon his eyes; and he looked intently and was restored, and saw everything clearly. And he sent him away to his home, saying, "Do not even enter the village."

Mk. viii. 22–6.

Hints and Signs by the Messiah

Throughout His whole ministry Jesus tried to make it clear to His disciples that He was the true Messiah who had been sent by God to gather and redeem His people, the true Israel. At first He could not make this claim too publicly because He knew it would rouse in Palestine both wild excitement and intense and sinister opposition to Him from the start, and He did not want this. It was necessary for Him to have not too much stir around Him so that His disciples might be able to think honestly and quietly about His teaching and person and ministry without being forced to make any premature decisions. Therefore He did not make many definite assertions about Himself in public. But in various ways He spoke and acted so that those who were willing to give Him their minds and wills, and to allow themselves to come quietly to the truth about Him should be able to discover who He really was and to learn more about Him, while the unreliable elements in public opinion were kept safely in the dark about this wonderful thing that was happening so quietly and graciously in their midst.

Therefore, instead of saying openly and plainly in so many words, "I am the Messiah sent by God to bring in His Kingdom," He rather lived out in the details of His life the part which the Messiah promised in the Old Testament was meant to play when He came. He gave mere hints in His teaching, and signs in His actions, which if they were read correctly should convince and thrill His real disciples, but yet arouse no undue suspicions in the minds of the outsider.

One of these signs, for instance, was His choice of the twelve Apostles. A Jew of Jesus's day who was seeking and waiting for the Messiah would see in this appointment of the twelve a claim that Jesus had come to restore the twelve tribes of Israel, as their Messiah. But for the outsider it would have little significance. His miracles of healing were also signs that He was the Messiah, for the Messiah was to be One who would heal the blind and the lame and the deaf (Is. xxxv. 5–6, LXI. 1–2; Lk. IV. 18; Mt. XI. 5). Other miracles were also signs. For instance, it was foretold in the Old Testament that when the Messiah came He would hold a banquet with His people on earth which would be a preliminary to the great Messianic banquet in the restored Kingdom of God (Is. xxv. 6, LXV. 13). When Jesus fed the five thousand in the wilderness, therefore, He was saying clearly to whoever could understand, that He was none other than this Messiah. Even a miracle such as the raising of the widow's son at Nain was highly significant. Nain was Shunem, the place where Elisha had raised the only son of the Shunammite woman. Jesus had impressed on His disciples' minds that John the Baptist His predecessor was the new Elijah the forerunner of the Messiah. Now in the new miracle at Shunem He is reminding them of this, and indicating that He Himself is indeed the true successor of Elijah. His final entry into Jerusalem, riding upon an ass, was one of His final signs of His Messiahship which everyone was expected to recognise.

In such quiet, almost secret, ways, then, Jesus tried by hints and signs, even early in His ministry, to convey to His disciples' minds the great divine mystery of who He was.

THE DEAF AND BLIND DISCIPLES

By the time the incidents we are considering here had taken place, the disciples should have understood. It should have dawned on them that Jesus was indeed the Messiah. If they had had eyes to see it they should by now have seen it. If they had had the ears to hear they should by now have heard it. But the words that He later spoke to Philip, "Have I been with you so long, and yet you do not know me, Philip?" (Jn. xiv. 9) applied at this time to everyone of these twelve men. Only occasionally had some of them been able to glimpse at flashes of His glory (Lk. v. 8), but the whole truth had not yet sunk into their minds as it should. They were still deaf and blind to the hints He had given them in His actions.

At the particular period when these two miracles of the healing of the deaf-mute at Decapolis and of the blind man at Bethsaida took place Jesus was deeply saddened by this stupidity and obtuseness on the part of His disciples. The whole section from Mk. vi–viii from which these stories are taken is punctuated by His sighs of disappointment over them, and by His complaints about their dullness and lack of understanding (Mk. vii. 18, viii. 17). He was at that period doing His greatest miracles; feeding the thousands, walking on the water, stilling the storms, but instead of believing and understanding, they merely gaped with wonder and amazement. Mark's comment on their behaviour at this time was, "They did not understand . . . but their hearts were hardened" (Mk. vi. 52).

As we preach and teach the Gospel within the Church we often find ourselves faced with the same deafness and blindness, the same inward lack of understanding as caused Jesus such distress and agony in His dealings with His own disciples. It is a difficulty that confronted the Apostles as they went out everywhere preaching and teaching, and it has been with the Church in every age. The people to whom we speak, whether they be old or young, educated or uneducated, rich or poor, are often like these deaf and blind disciples of Jesus in their early days. They are not able by themselves to see or make any real living response to the great things we are pointing to when we tell them that the eternal God Himself became incarnate in the babe Jesus, that Jesus died on the cross to atone for our sins, that He rose again from the dead to give us new life, that in Him we ourselves are dead and risen and exalted to Heaven. It is obvious when we speak to men about all this, that of themselves they have not the eyes to see it. They have not the capacity to take in anything of its glorious meaning. They have not the faith to grasp it. They certainly may compliment us on what we say. They may even admire some of the things we say when we speak about the wonderful human personality of Jesus and the sublimity of much of His teaching. They may like our style of speaking. They may come back again to us for more of it. But the essential meaning of what we say in many cases does not register on them, for there is nothing in them on which it can register. When it comes to the real heart of the Gospel, the real Word that demands full surrender and offers salvation and new life, they are like Peter and the rest of them in their deafness and blindness.

THE GIFT OF HEARING AND SIGHT

In the midst of this period of anxious tension between Jesus and His disciples, described in the central chapters of Mark's Gospel, He did two things to shame them about this lack of understanding on their part. Instead of giving them fresh signs of His Messiahship, He gave them two signs in which He showed them how hard a job He was having to make them hear what He was trying to say, and see what He was trying to signify.

"*And they brought to him a man who was deaf and had an impediment in his speech; and they besought him to lay his hand upon him. And taking him aside from the multitude privately, he put his fingers into his ears, and he spat and touched his tongue; and looking up to heaven, he sighed and said to him, 'Ephphatha,' that is, 'Be opened.' And his ears were opened, his tongue was released, and he spoke plainly.*"

"*And they came to Bethsaida. And some people brought to him a blind man, and begged him to touch him. And he took the blind man by the hand and led him out of the village; and when he had spit on his eyes and laid his hands upon him, he asked him, 'Do you see anything?' And he looked up and said, 'I see men; but they look like trees, walking.' Then again he laid his hands upon his eyes; and he looked intently and was restored, and saw everything clearly.*"

Both these miracles have certain important features in common. In both cases Jesus leads His man apart from the crowd in order to heal him. In both cases He uses spittle. In both cases He has to make a troublesome effort to effect the cure. In the case of the deaf man He sighs and looks to heaven, and with the blind man He has to repeat His treatment again before He can have full success. The healing in this case is a gradual process in contrast with so many of His other miracles.

Jesus meant the disciples to see themselves both in this deaf man and this blind man. What He was trying to do for these men in the physical realm, in taking them apart and agonising over them, He was trying to do for His disciples by taking them apart from the crowds and spending His care and prayer upon them. Let them look at Him and take this in and see what their continued deafness and blindness was costing Him in sighs and effort of body and soul.

It is significant, too, that immediately after these two miracles the disciples began to be able to hear and to see and to believe the hidden testimony that Jesus was giving to Himself in His teaching and miracles. The spiritual miracle began to take place within them. He took His disciples again apart from the crowds to Caesarea Philippi, and He asked Peter directly, "Who do you say that I am?" And Peter replied, "You are the Christ, the Son of the living God." Here a miracle had happened indeed. The inward spiritual power to see what He had been trying to show to Peter from the start of their friendship had at last been given him as a wonderful gift from God. "Blessed are you, Simon Bar-Jona," Jesus exclaimed. "For flesh and blood has not revealed this to you but my Father who is in heaven" (Mt. xvi. 15–17). The Word He had been speaking for such a long time to Peter had at last by the grace of God penetrated his soul. He now had the power to hear it. The Christ of the Gospels not only gave light for men to see, He also gave men the power to see and appreciate the light. He not only spoke the Word of God, He also gave the hearing and understanding of the Word of God as His own miraculous gift to men.

Christ can work the same inward miracle in the minds and hearts of those who hear His Gospel preached and taught today, and yet are blind to its real meaning and deaf to its true significance. This is what makes our otherwise almost impossible task in teaching and preaching full of possibility and hope. At the end of His life Jesus spoke to His disciples about the works they had seen Him do, referring to His miracles of physical healing. And then He spoke about "greater works" which His disciples could now be able to do in His name because He was going to ascend to His Father (Jn. xiv. 12). What were these "greater works" which His disciples were now to be able to accomplish? Is Jesus not referring to the miracle of giving minds that are spiritually blind the eyes to see the Kingdom of God, the miracle of making people who have no capacity for God suddenly come to have it? This is a miracle greater and more wonderful than any miracle in the physical realm. And as we work in the name of Christ we are able to accomplish this miracle in His name because He has gone to the Father, and from where He has gone He sends upon us and all His people the Holy Ghost, His own creative Spirit of Life which entering the hearts of men can give them new faculties, make them creatures of a new world, able now to be born into, to grasp and live in the new dimension of the Kingdom of God, the new world of the glory of God that has already broken into our midst with the coming of Jesus.

This miracle of inward hearing and sight is the peculiar work of the Holy Spirit within the Church today. After the Resurrection Jesus came to His disciples and breathed on them and said, "Receive the Holy Spirit" (Jn. xx. 22). This was a sign that He Himself in His risen power can now work this inward miracle of giving men inward life and sight and understanding. In Himself He gives us not only the Light, but also the power to see it. This is what we confess and rejoice in when we thank God that Jesus not only lived and died and rose again, but after He ascended also sent the Holy Ghost upon His Church. When Jesus claimed in the Synagogue at Capernaum that He was the One who had come to give the "recovering of sight to the blind," He was not thinking only of His power to give physical sight but of His power to enable men to see and appreciate and enter the Kingdom of God which He had brought near.

PATIENCE, TACT AND AGONY

We are meant always to remember how difficult Jesus found it to cure the spiritual insensitivity of which we have been speaking. The evidence of the Gospels is that Jesus found the actual concrete physical blindness which confronted Him amongst the diseased crowds around Him, easier to cure than the spiritual blindness which confronted Him in His otherwise healthy disciples. He found it easier to accomplish physical miracles than the inward spiritual miracle we have been discussing here. Sometimes His physical cures, however, presented difficulties which taxed His patience and love a good deal. The two miracles before us here are examples of this. But it is precisely these two most arduous of His purely physical miracles that are used by Him to illustrate the greater difficulty He had in curing the spiritual blindness and deafness of His disciples.

Both these stories are a warning to us about the trouble we ourselves may need to take, and the patience and love we may need to exert, in trying to make other people see what we see in Jesus, and hear what we hear in His Word. In our work of teaching and preaching for this end, we are meant to copy Him as we see Him here. We are meant to notice how He took both men apart from the crowd and gave them each by themselves a quite individual and sympathetic treatment. We must do the same ourselves, giving careful pastoral care to each individual with his own peculiar problems and needs. We are meant to notice how He descended almost to the level of the blind man's superstition by using spittle to smear on his eyes. This was the kind of technique an ignorant man expected from a miracle worker, and Jesus stooped to encourage his faith by such a method. Is there nothing more we ourselves can do in trying to come down to the level of quite simple and ignorant people in order to help them to understand the Word of God? We are meant also to notice how in the case of the blind man Jesus stopped half-way through the cure and asked him if he saw anything. Are we not meant to make the same loving and careful examination of the progress people are making under us? We are meant to notice how in this case too, He looked up to heaven and sighed. Though God alone could do this miracle, yet its accomplishment deeply involved His own human agency and suffering. Is this not an encouragement to us to agonise more in prayer for those whom we are trying to bring to sight and hearing? Perhaps even from Jesus's use of spittle in these miracles we are meant to take the lesson which the early fathers took—that it was only by imparting something of Himself to men that He could cure them. Are we not called to a similar imparting of ourselves to others on our own level? We are certainly meant to notice that the cure in each case came fairly slowly. We must learn that this wonderful gift of the power to see and understand and grasp spiritual things does not always show itself quickly as it comes to men. Therefore the more do we need patience and tact and imagination and agonising love in our dealings with each other within the Church.

Growth towards Clarity

The blind man was cured in two distinct stages. Jesus first of all restored him to sight. He anointed his eyes and asked him if he saw anything. The blind man looked up and said, "*I see men, but they look like trees, walking.*" The blind man could now indeed see. But everything was vague and without its true form, and he honestly confessed that his sight was still imperfect. Christ then helped him to come to clarity of vision. "*He laid his hands again upon his eyes; and he looked intently and was restored, and saw everything clearly.*"

This often happens in the Church today when people begin to gain their spiritual sight. Many soon reach a half-way stage. They begin to see indeed. They become dimly aware of realities around them that they never sensed before. They know that there is a new spiritual realm in Jesus Christ. There is the light of eternity shining on them in His face. The Kingdom of God is now real to them. But they have no clarity. They are unable to think out the implications of their faith or to see the connexions properly between one thing they see and another thing. Everything is vague and jumbled, even though they can see.

Some people remain like this all their days, content to see vaguely and to know vaguely. But this is not a healthy state for a Christian. If we are to grow in strength and usefulness in the service of Christ we must also grow in clarity of conviction. Growth in the grace of Christ is accompanied by growth in the knowledge of Christ (Pet. III. 18). We must seek, then, by discussing our faith with others, by reading the Bible and Christian books, to allow our faith to become more and more coherent, and our convictions to become more and more clear and articulate. It is not easy to pursue this course. But our great encouragement to do so must lie in the fact that clarity as well as sight depends on an inward gift given to us by Jesus Christ Himself. He can not only work within our minds and hearts the miracle of enabling us to see, but also that of enabling us to come to see things clearly.

THE EPILEPTIC BOY

And when they came to the disciples, they saw a great crowd about them, and scribes arguing with them. And immediately all the crowd, when they saw him, were greatly amazed, and ran up to him and greeted him. And he asked them, "What are you discussing with them?" And one of the crowd answered him, "Teacher, I brought my son to you, for he has a dumb spirit; and wherever it seizes him, it dashes him down; and he foams and grinds his teeth and becomes rigid; and I asked your disciples to cast it out, and they were not able." And he answered them, "O faithless generation, how long am I to be with you? How long am I to bear with you? Bring him to me." And they brought the boy to him; and when the spirit saw him, immediately it convulsed the boy, and he fell on the ground and rolled about, foaming at the mouth. And Jesus asked his father, "How long has he had this?" And he said, "From childhood. And it has often cast him into the fire and into the water, to destroy him; but if you can do anything, have pity on us and help us." And Jesus said to him, "If you can! All things are possible to him who believes." Immediately the father of the child cried out and said, "I believe; help my unbelief!" And when Jesus saw that a crowd came running together, he rebuked the unclean spirit, saying to it, "You dumb and deaf spirit, I command you, come out of him, and never enter him again." And after crying out and convulsing him terribly, it came out, and the boy was like a corpse; so that most of them said, "He is dead." But Jesus took him by the hand and lifted him up, and he arose. And when he had entered the house, his disciples asked him privately, "Why could we not cast it out?" And he said to them, "This kind cannot be driven out by anything but prayer."

Mk. ix. 14–29.

Public failure in the name of Christ

Here for the first time we see the disciples failing miserably before the public. They had, of course, had many previous failures in their discipleship of Jesus. They had disappointed Him many a time. But never before had they been involved in such a desperate and humiliating situation of open public failure.

They had not expected it. Some time before, Jesus had given them power to heal diseases and cast out devils in His name. "And he called to him the twelve and began to send them out

two by two, and gave them authority over the unclean spirits"
(Mk. VI. 7). They went out in obedience to His commission and
they found that the power He had given them really worked.
"So they went out and preached that men should repent. And
they cast out many demons, and anointed with oil many that
were sick and healed them" (Mk. VI. 12–13). It was a wonderful
experience of success. They were excited and exultant when they
saw miracle after miracle taking place as they obeyed Jesus's
instructions and commands. It was thrilling to be able in the
name of Jesus to go into this world so full of bondage and
misery to bring relief and liberty, and to solve the deepest
problems of life for their fellow men.

But now they had to learn that it is not always a plain path
of triumph and glory that we tread when we enlist in the service
of Jesus. Jesus had gone up to the top of a nearby mountain
with Peter and James and John. Afterwards they learned that
on that mountain top He had undergone a momentary transfiguration. Peter and James and John had seen His body become radiant with heavenly light, had seen Him in this state
talking with Moses and Elijah, and had heard a voice from a
cloud saying, "This is my beloved son, listen to him" (Mk. IX.
7). All that they knew at the time, however, was that He had
gone up there for prayer, and had left them down below to
carry on His mission as best they could.

They did what they could during His absence. We can
imagine them giving alms to the beggars, teaching inquirers
what Jesus said about God and Himself and life, and curing
one or two very ordinary cases of sickness or possession brought
to them.

And then this extremely difficult case was brought at a very
awkward time, and there was a most humiliating scene. What
happened at the foot of that mountain so impressed itself on
their memory and was talked about so much afterwards that
we have in the Gospels a very full and detailed account of it.

Some scribes from Jerusalem obviously out to make trouble
came along to mix with the crowds who were looking for Jesus.
He was by this time beginning to be slightly unpopular and
these scribes were trying to make things as difficult as they
could in order to destroy His influence with the people. The
disciples were no doubt annoyed and uncomfortable to see

them arriving to spoil their peace, especially when Jesus was not there to answer and silence them.

Just as the scribes arrived, a father came with a sick child who was subject to fearful and quickly recurring epileptic fits. He told the disciples the tragic story of how the little lad was now seized frequently by the devil and thrown into insane convulsions, of how he could never be left alone for a minute, for he was always trying to commit suicide by throwing himself into fire or water. Could they not do something? There was the child lying possessed and helpless at their feet!

They did their best, and at first they were fairly confident. They did what Jesus had told them to do. They went through the proper ritual and uttered the proper formula. They challenged the evil spirit in the name of Jesus. But nothing happened. The case was beyond their power.

The crowd began to jeer, and the scribes seized their opportunity there and then to prove that Jesus was an impostor. They were educated and naturally clever men, these scribes, and though the disciples tried to stand up for their master, they had little skill in arguing, and the proof of their impotence was there lying at their feet. The evidence was plainly against them. The name of Jesus on their lips had failed. Here was something He had professed His name able to do, and yet it had proved inadequate. They themselves in their bewilderment must have been tempted to doubt. It was a shattering and utterly humiliating experience. They stood before the crowd powerless, ridiculous, almost ashamed.

Does this scene not remind us forcibly of our own situation in the Church today? Time and again the accusation is levelled against us that the Church has failed and that our failure is obvious! We can hear ourselves accused on every side for our impotence to do what Jesus has obviously commissioned us to do in His name. We should be able in the name of Jesus to cast out the devils from the hearts of men—the devils that break up homes, that warp men's personalities and drive them to delinquency and crime and disorderliness. Many in the world look to us to provide some sign that the name of Jesus Christ is still powerful to accomplish such miracles within the social life of a country. But there are few signs that there is any such power available for men today. The devils are not being cast out, crime figures are soaring, and increasing juvenile delinquency becomes part of the accepted pattern of life. We are failing in our day and generation to speak a word that is indeed the power of God unto salvation, and that has all the cleansing and renewing effects that Christ has promised to attach to His Word in every generation. The tragedy of this situation is deepened by the fact that there are within the fellowship of the Church so many who like this father come into our midst with a simple faith that the Church is indeed the place into which they can come with their worst problems and heaviest burdens and find relief and release and power. Yet our word does not seem to have the power they have come to seek in it. We have no real answer to the accusing voice of our critics, for the proof of our impotence is irrefutable. It is to be seen not only in the state of the world as it lies around about our doors but also far too often in the state of the ordinary Church member who sits in our pews. He regularly listens to our word—a word that claims to be the Word of the Lord, and yet it appears to make not the slightest difference in the way he lives his life from day to day.

THE PROMISE OF HIS RETURN

There was only one saving feature in the pitiful situation in which the disciples found themselves. They expected Jesus to come back to them, and they expected Him soon. As they disputed with the scribes and spoke encouraging words to the disappointed, despairing father, their eyes wandered often up the mountainside where they had seen Him disappearing a few hours before, and they strained to see if He was now coming down. This was what made them hold on, and saved them from admitting final defeat. Their hope was in Jesus alone. He had promised to come back to them. They believed He would come and they knew from experience that He never came too late.

They felt, too, that it was Jesus's responsibility now to come and take control of this situation. After all, it was Jesus who had involved them in all this trouble. It was because they had tried to be faithful to Him that they now found themselves in this sorry plight. It was because they had tried to be faithful to Him that all this public shame and ridicule had come their way. Certainly their efforts to obey His Word had been poor and fumbling, but it was His work they had been doing, His battle they had been fighting. Therefore it was His failure they were involved in. It was His enemies they were facing in these scribes. If they knew Him at all, they felt He was bound not to fail them in what was an hour of crisis and need, both for Him and for them. They knew that the moment He came, their failure would be turned into victory.

We ourselves today are entitled to have the same thoughts. For, indeed, our main reason for having hope and confidence as we face our situation in the world today is simply the fact that Jesus Christ has promised to come into our midst, and He will never desert those who look to Him. He will come, and when He comes, our whole situation will be different. Surely, we can argue, He is bound to come! It is His battle we are fighting, not our own. It is through obeying His command that we have found ourselves undertaking the tasks that bring us into publicity as His representatives, that involve us in our failures and thus show up our deficiencies in such a vivid way before the watching world. We can carry on His work and risk our failures, and face the reproaches and sneers they involve us in, if we never fail in our confidence that Jesus Christ who has ascended to the right hand of God and to whom all power is now given in heaven and on earth will never desert those who look up to Him. We can be strong in the expectancy that He will come down from His glory into the midst of all our most humiliating situations to win the day in favour of those who are taking up His cause and suffering defeat and reproach in His place.

Before Jesus finally left His disciples to ascend to His Father's throne and glory, He gave the promise to them, "when I go and prepare a place for you, I will come again and will take you to myself, that where I am you may be also" (Jn. xiv. 3). This promise, like many others in John's Gospel, refers not only to Jesus's final return in glory at the end of the world, but also to an often repeated return of Jesus from His glory into the midst of the Church. Because we expect Him often to fulfil this promise, we gather in Church on Sundays and lift up our eyes in worship to the exalted Christ, the Lamb in the midst of the heavenly throne. But we lift up our eyes in this way because we also expect His coming into our midst to take fresh control of His church and of ourselves in all our inadequacy and failure. Jesus will fulfil this pledge to His Church. "Where two or three are gathered in my name, there am I in the midst of them" (Mt. xviii. 20). He will come into our midst wherever we are truly looking up to Him, and at the same time seeking to tackle in His name the problems that we face in the mission He has given us in this world. We cannot command His presence or force Him to come, but we can always remind ourselves and Him of His promise to keep tryst with us, and we can turn our eyes, as the disciples did, in the direction from which we expect Him to come. Our sole hope for the Church, for the power and wisdom we need to make our work effective, lies not in ourselves, not in our fresh resolutions and plans and new techniques, but simply in His promise to come again into our midst and in His fulfilment of that promise in His good time.

The Lord in the Midst

He came down from the glory of His transfiguration experience into their midst with serene majesty. They noticed a strange heavenly radiance about Him, for His experience of exaltation had not yet fully passed. To those in the crowd who had eyes to see there was something more majestic and glorious about Him than they had ever before noticed. "*And immediately all the crowd, when they saw him, were greatly amazed, and ran up to him and greeted him.*" How majestically He acted and spoke! In no time He thrust Himself into the centre and took command. He directed the battle to Himself and away from His disciples. "*What are you discussing with them?*" he asked the crowd, and He commanded that the child should be brought to Him. He comes on the scene as One in whose presence nothing is now "impossible." "*All things are possible to him who believes,*" is His serene word to the poor half-disbelieving father.

Yet in spite of this majestic radiance He was still the same gentle and compassionate Master whom they have learned to trust so well. It was His love for them in their need that brought Him back down to the valley when He might have still remained up there on the mountain top in His glory. He might still have been listening to Moses and Elijah talking of His own passion and its meaning, but He had a sympathetic ear for the whole story of this problem child as the father poured it out to him tearfully and pleadingly. Perhaps the most touching feature of the whole story is in what happened in the middle of the cure when the little lad fell to the ground lifeless and limp—"*The boy was like a corpse; so that most of them said, 'He is dead.' But Jesus took him by the hand and lifted him up.*"

This is the Christ we can wait for with confidence as we hold fast till He comes to be with us in our battle and to help us to meet the desperate need of so many people who have come to depend on us, as they bring their problems and burdens into our midst. This Jesus Christ is the same today as yesterday—majestic yet meek and lowly, omnipotent and yet tender and understanding enough to stoop to the ground and lift us up by the hand, inspiring not only amazement and wonder at the glory He brings with Him but also a confidence that enables men to open their lives to Him and unburden before Him the whole sorry tale of their distresses and anxieties. This is the Christ who inspires us, in spite of our unbelief, to say "*I believe*," and at the same time to confess, and lay at his feet the unbelief that always mingles with our faith.

The word He spoke to the crowd as He came amongst them was as majestic and compassionate as His person and His bearing. "*O faithless generation,*" He cried, "*How long am I to be with you? How long am I to bear with you?*" We cannot understand what this cry means if we think of it simply as the cry of a disappointed and misunderstood prophet, exasperated at the unfaithfulness and slowness of the people he represents. On the contrary, what Jesus said in this utterance would have been sheer blasphemy had He been merely a great prophet or teacher. No prophet ever had the right to speak for himself as Jesus spoke in this word. It is a word too reminiscent of the loving utterances of God Himself throughout the Old Testament expressing the wounds of His heart (cf. Jer. viii. 21) over the children of Israel as they tried His patience, and He nevertheless decided not to give them up but to hold on to them no matter how much tribulation is to be involved (Is. vi. 11). "How can I give you up, O Ephraim! How can I hand you over, O Israel! How can I make you as Admah! How can I treat you like Zeboim! My heart recoils within me, my compassion grows warm and tender. I will not execute my fierce anger, I will not again destroy Ephraim; for I am God and not man, the Holy One in your midst" (Hos. xi. 8).

It was as the "Holy One in the midst" that Jesus cried, "*O faithless generation, how long am I to be with you?*" The cry "*how long*" refers not simply to the short ministry of Jesus Himself on earth amongst His disappointing disciples, not even to the span of His whole earthly life, but rather to the whole history of God's dealing with Israel throughout the long centuries. Jesus can speak in this way because, through a mystery we can understand only as dimly as we understand His transfiguration experience, He Himself is the Lord who ever was and is to come (Rev. i. 8 and 17). In His love and patience He is Jesus Christ, "the same yesterday and today and for ever" (Heb. xiii. 8). Spoken as they were immediately after His descent from the mount of transfiguration, His words here remind us that God in His mercy has chosen not to remain by Himself alone, keeping His glory and His fellowship to Himself, but wills to share them with men, no matter how long and costly the agony of doing this may be. Soon He was to give even clearer expression to this divine love, tried to the utmost yet never giving way: "O Jerusalem, Jerusalem, killing the prophets and stoning those who are sent to you! How often would I have gathered your children together as a hen gathers her brood under her wings, and you would not!"

PRACTICAL ADVICE

As the day was ending, when Jesus was alone with His disciples He spoke to them in practical terms about the reason for their failure. "*His disciples asked him privately, 'Why could we not cast it out?' And he said to them, 'This kind cannot be driven out by anything but prayer.'*" Not by anything! Not by a vigorous reformation of the Church's organisation, not by the adoption of the most up-to-date techniques, not by changing the language we use and the way we speak in preaching the Gospel, not by a fresh and more sympathetic psychological approach to those we are dealing with, "*not . . . by anything but prayer,*" and by prayer alone. Many reforms may be necessary, but the Church that neglects its prayer life will in the end of the day find itself through sheer disappointment forced again back on its knees in a prayer that trusts in Christ alone to do what nothing else can do. We have learned that Christ will never leave us alone with our failures, but we need not be content with our many failures. Jesus here reminds us that there are failures which can be avoided. The desperate needs of our people will be more certainly and fully met, the devils will be more quickly cast out, His Kingdom will come the sooner—if we pray.

THE COIN IN THE FISH'S MOUTH

When they came to Capernaum, the collectors of the half-shekel tax went up to Peter and said, "Does not your teacher pay the tax?" He said, "Yes." And when he came home, Jesus spoke to him first, saying, "What do you think, Simon? From whom do kings of the earth take toll or tribute? From their sons or from others?" And when he said, "From others," Jesus said to him, "Then the sons are free. However, not to give offence to them, go to the sea and cast a hook, and take the first fish that comes up, and when you open its mouth you will find a shekel; take that and give it to them for me and for yourself."

Mt. XVII. 24–27.

The Jewish authorities often became annoyed and offended at what Jesus did and said. To them it was a scandal that He should go about forgiving people their sins, and talking as if He were greater than Moses or the Temple or the Sabbath day. What next would He say or claim? They followed Him round and tried to trip Him up by asking questions to which they hoped He would give some answer that might later definitely compromise Him or give them grounds for ridiculing Him. On this particular occasion they made a flank attack on Peter when he was off his guard. Taxes were being collected, and they challenged him: "*Does not your teacher pay the tax?*" They put this question publicly, and there was malice and contempt in their minds as they asked it. They would test this Teacher. He had, in little ways, been talking and acting as if He were indeed different from the common run of teachers, scholars, and religious men. Now they wanted to press the issue. Was He prepared really to act up to His arrogant claim when it came to a real showdown with the powers that be? Did He pay taxes or not?

Peter fell into the trap with an answer that was too short and straightforward for such a subtle situation. "*Yes,*" he said, in the same way as we would say, "Of course." With this the discussion finished. It was a victory for the opposition. Jesus had been humiliated by His own disciple. In the eyes of the onlookers Peter had made a clear and simple confession that though His Master talked and sometimes acted in a lordly way, He nevertheless, when it came to a clear practical issue, was on the same level as everyone else, and had no more rights to any greater liberty than any other ordinary human being. In the way Peter said it, it could be taken to mean that Jesus was bound to pay taxes, and owed as a matter of course the same tribute to earthly rulers as did any other man.

Simon Peter seems at this moment completely to have forgotten what had been revealed to him at Caesarea Philippi only a day or two previously. Then he had said to Jesus, "Thou art the Christ, the Son of the living God" (Mt. xvi. 16), and Jesus had called him by his new name, Peter, and called him blessed by God. Peter seems also to have forgotten his very recent experience on the mount of transfiguration when he had seen the divine glory of the Kingdom of God shining in Jesus in a way that belonged to no mere human being. If Peter had pondered these experiences, as he should, he would never have answered such a simple and glib "*Yes,*" to the question, "*Does not your teacher pay the tax?*" It was a humiliating failure in Simon's discipleship. He had let down His Master in front of His enemies.

In the incident which took place the same evening, Jesus put His disciple right on this most important practical point. Though Jesus was present when Simon humiliated Him by his foolish answer, He had remained silent. Like a wise parent dealing with a difficult child, He waited till He had time quietly to broach the subject in private when a suitable occasion arose. He took His opportunity the same evening when the public had all withdrawn. "*What do you think, Simon?*" He asked, "*From whom do kings of the earth take toll or tribute? From their sons or from others?*" He reverted to Peter's old name— Simon—for Peter had been playing again the old unbelieving part of Simon. Simon Peter in this question was asked to suppose that His Master had been a king's son—a prince of the blood royal. What now about the question put to him by the Pharisees? How should he have answered them if Jesus had been an earthly prince? Do earthly kings take tribute from their own families, or submit their own children to the humiliating annoyances of petty tax collectors? Or do they not confine such sign of bondage to those outside their own family circle?

Peter immediately gave Jesus the only possible answer. Kings tax only their subjects but never their children. Jesus said to him, "*Then the sons are free.*"

Thus was Peter rebuked. How foolish he had been, one day to give his teacher a title to which all earthly homage is due, "Thou are the Christ, the Son of the living God," and the next day to suggest that the same Christ, the Son of God, owed submission when an earthly tax gatherer on behalf of a petty authority—even were it the Emperor of Rome itself—demanded what he thought were his dues. Peter had confessed Christ as Lord, but had failed to keep the Lordship of His Master before his mind as he faced the day-to-day problems that came before him in the service of His Master. Poor Peter! He could rise to great heights of vision and faith and profession of loyalty, but he could, very soon after, come crashing down to a ridiculously low level.

Then came this rather strange command of Jesus, and the miracle which followed it. Jesus said to him, "*Then the sons are free. However, not to give offence to them, go to the sea and cast a hook, and take the first fish that comes up, and when you open its mouth you will find a shekel; take that and give it to them for me and for yourself.*"

There are those who feel that this miracle story is of such an unusual type to find in the Gospels that it cannot have any genuine basis in the life of Jesus. Most of the other miracles of Jesus, they say, fit into the character of One who made His miraculous power always subservient to loving compassion. But in this story they find a display of miraculous power given for what they regard as a trivial end, and a mere sensational display of commonplace wizardry and magic. They therefore regard this story as a poor attempt on the part of some primitive writer in the early Church to give some convincing proof that Jesus indeed had great divine power. To read a profound lesson here is to read what they think was never intended to be there.

But we must not take offence at the simple way in which God sometimes "babbles," as Calvin puts it, to men when He is seeking to teach them the meaning of His divine Word. This miracle is so remarkable and profound in its meaning as a sign that it would be a pity to be too proud to learn from it.

THE SIGN OF MAJESTY IN THE MIDST OF HUMILIATION

Jesus paid the tax that, through Peter's folly, had now become such a humiliating issue between Himself and the Jewish authorities. But as He did so, He gave privately to His disciples a majestic sign of His Lordship. He paid His tax in the most lordly manner any tax has ever been paid. "*Go to the sea and cast a hook, and take the first fish that comes up, and when you open its mouth you will find a shekel; take that and give it to them.*" He made the sea pay His tribute, for He was Lord of earth and sea, and in making the sea pay such tribute to earthly authority, He makes it pay tribute to His own Lordship. The disciples could never have forgotten this sign.

But it was a sign to them alone. The authorities who took the shekel knew nothing of its source. Outwardly to the world Christ was this good yet insignificant teacher who in spite of His great claims must be careful how He walks. "He was in the world, and the world was made through Him, yet the world knew Him not" (Jn. i. 10). Yet while the world thinks this of Him, the disciples are given a hidden sign by which they know that He is the Lord of whom it is written, "In his hands are the depths of the earth; the heights of the mountains are his also. The sea is his for he made it" (Ps. xcv. 4–5). Even today Jesus continues to perform such signs of His Lordship to His disciples alone, and not to the world. When we stand before worldly authority or criticism in the name of Christ, we have very little to show to prove that His great and majestic claims are true. The Church must pay its taxes. It must take its place in the life of a state amongst a row of other very earthly and ordinary human institutions none of which claims to have such a divine origin and life. In many ways it has to pay a certain outward homage to earthly rule. Yet in the midst of all this, and in spite of all this, there are many within the Church to whom Jesus Christ has given, as He gave to Peter, hidden, quiet, yet unmistakable signs that He is Lord of all. In answer to prayers, in the provision of their human needs, in the providence that brings men out of darkness into light and out of death into life, Christ has proved to them in many subtle and quiet ways that all things are in His hands, the seas, the minds and purposes of men, the financial currents of the world's life, even the principalities and powers of darkness. "Yet a little while, and the world will see me no more, but you will see me" (Jn. XIV.19).

This we must remember from day to day, especially in those moments when we have to give an answer for Jesus before men, as Peter had to give an answer to the Jewish authorities. In shaping the policy and attitude of the Church towards human authority we must never forget that in Christ we serve One to whom all nations and all men owe tribute. Therefore though the Church must always suffer humiliation, let us never, from an excessive desire to be modest, inflict on Jesus Christ any unnecessary humiliation to His name on the part of His own disciples. The world will not necessarily believe in Him. But it is tragedy indeed if the world receives the impression that the Church itself does not believe in His Lordship, and therefore does not assert His claims. It is tragedy indeed when the world sees professing Christians living gloomy and depressed lives and hears them uttering little else than pessimistic forebodings of the future. Such a way of life on our part is no less a slight on the Lordship of Christ than was Peter's humiliating answer to the Jewish authorities. We cannot be expected to cultivate an artificial psychological sheen in order to advertise the supposed radiance of the Christian life, but we can at least have some signs around us, that here Jesus Christ is still proving to His people that He is Lord.

THE SIGN OF HUMILIATION IN THE MIDST OF MAJESTY

Yet however zealously we must seek to assert the Lordship of Christ, it is of deep significance that at exactly the same time as He gave the sign of His Lordship, He showed Himself willing to remain in His state of lowliness and humiliation. Jesus paid His tax under circumstances that were humiliating to His reputation. In order "*not to give offence to them*" Peter was sent to pay the shekel. He must now go and act as if His Master were the servant and subject of all men.

In order not to give offence to men it was inevitable that Jesus should manifest His glory not simply in spectacular signs of lordly self-assertion but also in true humiliation and weakness. If He had refused to stoop to pay taxes in order to manifest His free gracious love, would He not also by the same decision have refused to stoop to wash His disciples feet, to submit to the nails that fixed Him to the cross, to the wearing of the crown of thorns—and all of us would have been indeed offended, for we could not be saved from evil. In order to save, rather than to offend, He was content to become "flesh," to put on an ordinary appearance and live a life of humiliation.

Lest other men be offended and put beyond the possibility of salvation we must always be prepared, if need be, to show a weak and humiliated aspect to those who are outside. Often we have to manifest the glory of Christ by being and remaining utterly without dignity. Otherwise we cannot truly represent Him before men. If we are going to represent Christ before men, sometimes we have to be content simply to appear to be weak, and thus share in His humiliation as completely as possible. Jesus, as well as being Lord, was also a very humble, ordinary, approachable man born to a carpenter in Nazareth. How can men come to know His love and thus His true dignity unless they see something also of this aspect of Christ in us and in His Church? Therefore though we ourselves know Christ as Lord, and see the Church as the glorious temple of the living God of which He is the chief corner-stone, let us not be ashamed to play our part as the servants of men and the servants of earthly states, to pay our taxes, to line up in the procession alongside of every other invited organisation on civil and national occasions. The Church of Jesus Christ must often take a place and play a part which seems incommensurable with the true glory of Jesus Christ. The world may sometimes misunderstand the humiliation we submit to in His name. It is not a pleasant experience for us to have our Christian patience taken as a sign of weakness rather than of love. But the world would misunderstand more seriously and men would be offended if we tried to withdraw from our humble part. In this humiliation there is revealed the true glory of Jesus Christ. A Church that tries to reflect the Lordliness of Christ and to manifest His greatness in any other way than through His humiliation and lowliness, misrepresents Him before men, and offends the world instead of saving it.

THE SIGN OF LOVE WITHIN HIS HUMBLE MAJESTY

Jesus associated Peter with Himself in the debt He paid that day. The shekel was to be paid not only for Himself but "*for me and for yourself*," He said to Peter. Perhaps this as a parable of His life. All His life He lived paying a debt—the debt of those He had come to live with and stand by and take as His people and His friends and kinsmen. Because He identified Himself with us in this way He had to pay a humiliating price of suffering all His days and in the end the fearful agony of the Cross. But in paying all this for us He pays what only He can pay.

It is worthwhile noticing how He associated Peter with Himself not only in His debt but in His regal privileges. When He asserted His freedom and Lordship to Peter that day, He did not say merely, "Then am I free." He said, "*Then the sons are free.*" Not only does He pay Peter's debt but He associates Peter with His divine Sonship and royal liberty.

What He pays for Himself He pays not for Himself but for us. What He wins for Himself He wins not for Himself but for us. And in entering His fellowship and companionship we too share in the glorious liberty and royal privileges that belong indeed to the Children of God. "All things are yours, whether Paul or Apollos or Cephas or the world or life or death or the present or the future, all are yours; and you are Christ's; and Christ is God's" (1 Cor. III. 21–23).

THE WOMAN WITH A
SPIRIT OF INFIRMITY

Now he was teaching in one of the synagogues on the sabbath. And there was a woman who had had a spirit of infirmity for eighteen years; she was bent over and could not fully straighten herself. And when Jesus saw her, he called her and said to her, "Woman, you are freed from your infirmity." And he laid his hands upon her, and immediately she was made straight, and she praised God. But the ruler of the synagogue, indignant because Jesus had healed on the sabbath, said to the people, "There are six days on which work ought to be done; come on those days and be healed, and not on the sabbath day." Then the Lord answered him, "You hypocrites! Does not each of you on the sabbath untie his ox or his ass from the manger, and lead it away to water it? And ought not this woman, a daughter of Abraham whom Satan bound for eighteen years, be loosed from this bond on the sabbath day?" As he said this, all his adversaries were put to shame; and all the people rejoiced at all the glorious things that were done by him.

Lk. XIII. 10–17.

A LIVING WORD REPLACES DEAD DOCTRINE

"Now he was teaching in one of the synagogues on the sabbath."

The ruler of the synagogue allowed Jesus to teach in it that day. Indeed, he may have actually invited Jesus to teach in it. He wanted his people to enjoy the best religious teaching of the day, and he regarded Jesus as a good religious teacher. It would be a good thing, he felt, for his congregation to have the fresh mental and emotional stimulus that could come from hearing a new popular voice. This helped to bring the people out to worship. People everywhere were flocking to listen to Jesus. It might deepen the spiritual life and sensibilities of his flock if he had Him as the visiting preacher for a Sabbath.

But he became shocked and angry, because, as Jesus taught, something quite startling actually happened. A woman's heart and soul and attitude, both physical and spiritual, were changed. This made him lose control of himself, and he finished up by interrupting Jesus and railing at the people for allowing such a thing to happen in their midst.

He had wanted Jesus to preach, but he hadn't wanted anything to happen as Jesus preached. He had wanted no upset in the usual quiet routine of teaching and listening and enjoying the preacher. He had expected the Word of God to create perhaps a mild flutter and a pleasant sensation as the preacher's new ideas and theories flew round in people's minds. He wanted no deep-seated disturbance in the lives of his people, or in the social or political or ecclesiastical structures of the day. For him, to preach about the Kingdom of God was to point forward to something glorious away in the distant future, and to stir up the hearts of his hearers to want it and to long for it and pray for it and dream about it.

But for Jesus, the Word of God was like dynamite. The Word of God was the Kingdom and power of God here and now in the midst of men and women. When Jesus spoke the Word of God He spoke about a new Kingdom that had already invaded the life of this world, and was already making available for men new and revolutionary powers that could vitally affect human character and human society. He spoke about the new and near presence of God to his people with a forgiving and cleansing love that was seeking with real and urgent pressure to invade men's hearts and minds and lives. He spoke about a new inward liberty that could here and now be given to men and that would ultimately find its expression in setting them free from all outward bondage. Such teaching was not a teaching of theories and ideas, but the proclamation of divine realities that were actually there and then present as He talked about them. In other words, Jesus came not only to speak about the Kingdom but to bring in the Kingdom through His own presence and words and acts. As He spoke about the Kingdom He also breathed on men the Spirit of power and new life and liberty and resurrection that belonged to the Kingdom.

But here in front of Him in the synagogue, listening to His teaching, was a woman whose life was being narrowed and rendered useless by a cruel bondage of spirit to which somehow she had become subject. Her body was bent almost double and she could not straighten herself. Her vision, her liberty of movement, her dealings with others, her attitude to life were all deeply affected by this condition she was in. Indeed, the story describes her malady as more a spiritual condition than a physical one. For eighteen years she had suffered this. Jesus saw in her remaining there an obvious denial of the reality of everything He had been speaking about. She was the victim of the Satanic power He had come to destroy with His Kingdom. How could He speak of the reality of such deliverance as He had brought, and not here and now bring to effect what He was proclaiming? *"And when Jesus saw her, He called her and said to her, 'Woman, you are freed from your infirmity.' And He laid His hands upon her, and immediately she was made straight, and she praised God."*

This is the kind of powerful and living Word the preaching of the Kingdom of God should become on Sundays in the Church today. We have no right to remain content in the Church with mere talk about a Kingdom of God that is not much more than a "happy land, far, far, away". One day as Jesus was speaking about the Kingdom, a Pharisee in the crowd shouted out, "Blessed is he who shall eat bread in the Kingdom of God." The man obviously was thinking of this Kingdom of God as a dim and distant possibility far away in the future of this earth, offering a happiness that could be merely dreamed about and sighed after. But Jesus, in reply, told the parable of the Great Supper, in which He described a man giving a great and rich banquet to his friends, first making everything ready, and then sending out his servants to those who had been invited, with the announcement, "Come; for all is now ready" (Lk. xiv. 15–17). That was His way of telling the Pharisees that with Himself in their midst the Kingdom of God was there and then in their midst in all its hidden fullness and power, with the urgent pressure of its life challenging their decision, and seeking to invade their hearts and alter their circumstances. Another day, as He was speaking to His disciples, He said, "If you know these things, blessed are you if you do them" (Jn. xiii. 17). It is blessed to hear and talk and know of the Kingdom only if the knowledge and power of it sends us out to live as it should inspire us to live. This is why Jesus also likened the preaching of the Word of the Kingdom to the sowing of seed in the ground, a seed with a spontaneous powerful life within itself that must be allowed a radical hold and a transforming growth within the situation into which it is cast. It is this also that is behind Paul's great words about the Gospel he preached. "I am not ashamed of the Gospel; it is the power of God for salvation to everyone who has faith" (Rom. i. 16).

This power of God does not manifest itself regularly today in remarkable physical cures as it did in the presence of Jesus. Nor does it necessarily manifest itself in the minds and hearts of its hearers in strong emotional outbursts, but it must always register in the minds and hearts and lives of those who receive it as a word that challenges and impels to action and change and practical decision in daily life. This was the kind of Word that was preached in the midst of the life of the early Church as we see it in the New Testament. Paul can remind the Corinthians that when he was with them his speech and his message were "not in plausible words of wisdom, but in demonstration of the Spirit and power" (1 Cor. ii. 4). This meant that things happened in the midst of the congregation as he preached, because the risen Jesus Himself came into their midst and became the preacher. Therefore when these early preachers spoke about the forgiveness of sins, Christ Himself offered and gave forgiveness. When they spoke about the Kingdom of God, the King came into their midst, and men entered it through Him. When they spoke about "glorious liberty of the children of God" (Rom. viii. 21), it was about something their hearers were meant to experience through the Word that was then being preached. And though for them the days gradually passed away when outward miracles of healing took place under the Word of God, this did not matter, since the inward miracles of grace that took place in their hearts and minds and souls became more and more evident and more and more powerful.

In this light we must constantly examine what passes in our midst as the preaching of the Word of God. Is it living Word, or is it dead doctrine?

THE LIVING WORD GIVES SPIRITUAL LIBERTY

The sight of this woman in front of Him, impoverished, bound and bent, was to Jesus a sign of the spiritual impotence, bondage and short-sightedness that can at times paralyse the life of the children of God. There is a passage in the Old Testament which vividly describes the people of God as being like a sleepy woman, bent down and grovelling on the earth.

Awake, awake,
put on your strength, O Zion;
put on your beautiful garments,
O Jerusalem, the holy city;
for there shall no more come unto you
the uncircumcised and the unclean.
Shake yourself from the dust, arise;
O captive Jerusalem;
loose the bonds from your neck,
O captive daughter of Zion.   (Is. L. 1–2).

There Zion or the Church is likened to a half-drunken woman grovelling almost naked in the dust, and only half-awake to the offer of the immediate liberty and wealth and glory that God wants to bestow upon her if she will only look up and believe and accept His Word for it. The sight of this woman must have reminded Jesus of this passage. Indeed, it is possible that He was preaching from this very passage. She was typical of what happens, in every age, to the people of God when they ignore His living Word, substitute dead doctrine for the power of His Kingdom, and allow themselves to become deprived of their glorious liberty. That is why Jesus addressed her there and then, and commanded her to rise and be free, and enabled her immediately to praise God. This cure was a sign of what He had come to do for the Church in His day and for the Church in every century including the twentieth. He had come to give liberty.

It is important for us to notice that there was nothing extremely serious about her condition. She was not in danger of going to Hell. When Jesus called her a *"daughter of Abraham,"* He meant that she was indeed a child of God, a woman of true faith. Some of us in our own language would call her a truly "born-again" Christian. She was spiritually in the light and not in darkness. She had some measure of freedom in her body too. She did not need to be carried about. Her liberty was restricted but not entirely destroyed. She was *"bound"* by Satan, as Jesus said, but she was certainly not entirely in the clutches of Satan or at his disposal. A *"daughter of Abraham"*, yet *"bound!"*

The story is sometimes told of how a Roman Emperor once

died when his successor was in prison, and circumstances so worked out that the new Emperor was brought up out of his cell and seated on the imperial throne. A crown was put on his head, but a smith could not be immediately found to cut through the fetters on his arms and legs, and there he sat crowned and glorious in his status, and yet at the same time bound by prisoner's chains. It is a strange picture, and yet it describes the spiritual state of some of us today. Our status is that of the Children of God, justified by faith in Jesus. But in our daily life we are "*bound*" and do not reflect the glory and freedom of our status.

The Church of God is being attacked all over the world by the powers of evil. In some countries it is subjected to fierce outward persecution, its leaders are imprisoned, and its activity is curbed by harsh laws. Thus the devil fulfils his role of a "roaring lion" (1 Pet. v. 8) in attacking the Church. But in other lands the devil goes to work more quietly in binding the children of God. He works within the Church itself, indeed within the lives of its members, as an unseen spiritual binding force that keeps Christ's redeemed men and women back from full and free service of their Lord in this world.

Do we not all of us experience to an extent these ties which bind us and prevent us from rising up to glorify our Redeemer with our lives? The Apostle John describes three of these bonds in his well-known warning to us about the "lust of the flesh and the lust of the eyes and the pride of life" (1 Jn. 1. 16). Our Lord Himself describes another two of the chains that prevent our Christian liberty in His warning about the "cares of the world and the delight in riches" (Mt. xii. 22). We could also add our own words of warning about the way in which men and women become restricted in their spiritual development and usefulness by fear of the opinion of the world, by the chains of self-centredness, by addictedness to sloth and pleasure. Anything, indeed, that prevents us from setting our minds on the things that are above (Col. iii. 3) and seeking first the Kingdom of God and His righteousness (Mt. vi. 33) is an evil bond from which Christ is always seeking to deliver His people. "If the Son makes you free, you will be free indeed" (Jn. viii. 36), said Jesus. This need not to be taken to mean that we can become sinless people on this earth. Sin will always dwell within us and involve us in a bitter and unpleasant struggle. We will always have the experience of conflict with our own nature which Paul describes at the end of the seventh chapter of Romans. "Wretched man that I am! Who will deliver me from this body of death? Thanks be to God through Jesus Christ our Lord" (Rom. VII. 24–25). But though sin always dwells within us it need not dominate over us. Liberty and victory can be ours through the living Word which Christ will ever come to speak to us, in calling us, as He did this woman, to arise and walk in newness of life and glorify God.

THE LIVING WORD BREAKS MEN'S BONDAGE TO DEAD TRADITION

There was another kind of bondage from which people in that synagogue had to be delivered. It was the Sabbath day, and many people were shocked at what had happened. They all felt that it was wrong for healing to be done in this way on the Sabbath day. And in the name of their sacred Sabbath traditions, the ruler of the synagogue protested.

"*The ruler of the synagogue, indignant because Jesus had healed on the Sabbath, said to the people, 'There are six days on which work ought to be done; come on those days and be healed, and not on the Sabbath day.*" And as he spoke many in that congregation nodded their heads and looked at Jesus with anger. This was their tradition, and He had broken it.

But their tradition did not arise from the Word of God. The book of Moses taught this about the Sabbath: "It is a sign for ever between me and the people of Israel that in six days the Lord made heaven and earth, and on the seventh day he rested, and was refreshed" (Ex. XXXI. 17). The Sabbath therefore was for God's rest and refreshment. But here was a woman beginning now to enter fully into His rest and refreshment. What could be more fitting than that this should happen on this particular day when God expected His people to cease from their work and seek to share His grace in such rest and refreshment? What, indeed, could bring more rest and refreshment to God?

Jesus replied to the ruler's protest by speaking another powerful Word.

"*You hypocrites,*" He said, "*Does not each of you on the Sabbath*

untie his ox or his ass from the manger, and lead it away to water it?
And ought not this woman, a daughter of Abraham, whom Satan bound
for eighteen years, be loosed from this bond on the Sabbath day?"

As He spoke these words a new and wonderful thing happened in the minds of many of His hearers. They were delivered from the bondage of their tradition. They saw for the first time how stupid they had been in this matter. They saw a new meaning in the Sabbath, and they saw how wrong some of their traditions about it had been. As Jesus said this, *"all his adversaries were put to shame: and all the people rejoiced at all the glorious things that were done by him."* Surely when Jesus was able to deliver the congregation like this from such bondage to their dead traditions He was doing a miracle even greater than He had already accomplished in the woman who was now praising God at His feet.

It is urgent that Jesus by His living Word in the Church today should be allowed to do this miracle for every congregation and every denomination. He once uttered a solemn word of warning to the Pharisees. "For the sake of your tradition," He said to them, "You have made void the Word of God" (Mt. xv. 6). Time and again "traditions" appear within Churches, congregations and denominations. These may have no firm basis in the Word of God, yet for a long time they may be good and healthy customs and ideas. But there may come a time when the living Word of God, speaking to the Church through the risen Christ and the holy Scriptures demands new actions, new ways, new obedience and a fresh start. Then the struggle comes between the living Word of God and dead or dying tradition. It is very tragic when Church people make void the living Word of God by clinging to dead tradition and refusing to give it up. It may be that in our day certain views of the sanctity of Presbyterianism, Episcopalianism, Congregationalism, both broad views and narrow views, may belong to dead and dying tradition. It may be that certain views of what the Bible is, both broad views and narrow views, may belong to dead and dying tradition, and Christ may be calling us to a new view and a new attitude. It may be that certain customs within our own congregations, which worked well fifty years ago now belong to a dead and dying tradition and prevent real progress under the guidance and power of the Word of

God. It may be that a certain way of approaching the outsider, of running youth work and sunday-school work belong to the same dead and dying traditions. We must listen carefully to whatever the living Word of God as it comes through the Bible is saying to us in face of our traditions. "He who has an ear let Him hear what the Spirit says to the Churches" (Rev. ii. 11), for in hearing this living Word from Christ, a fresh and wonderful miracle can indeed take place in our midst. We can be delivered from our dead and dying Church traditions.

THE TEN LEPERS

On the way to Jerusalem he was passing along between Samaria and Galilee. And as he entered a village, he was met by ten lepers, who stood at a distance and lifted up their voices and said, "Jesus, Master, have mercy on us." When he saw them he said to them, "Go and show yourselves to the priests." And as they went they were cleansed. Then one of them, when he saw that he was healed, turned back, praising God with a loud voice; and he fell on his face at Jesus' feet, giving him thanks. Now he was a Samaritan. Then said Jesus, "Were not ten cleansed? Where are the nine? Was no one found to return and give praise to God except this foreigner?" And he said to him, "Rise and go your way; your faith has made you well."

Lk. XVII. 11–19.

DISTANT HEALING

Most of the people for whom Jesus worked His wonderful cures were those with whom He first had close personal dealings. Often He talked with them for a little while beforehand. They explained their need. He spoke to them about His power, and the power of faith. He also gave them a special word to encourage their hope. Then the miracle happened.

But this miracle of the cleansing of the ten lepers is a miracle of distant healing. It shows us how a group of men were blessed and cured by Jesus without their coming near to Him personally. They *"stood at a distance"* and shouted their request. The story is definite in asserting that most of these men came no nearer to Him in affection or devotion, and entered no closer a personal relationship with Him than most of the curious crowds who followed Him round for the mere excitement of the thing. Yet a miracle of His power was worked in their lives. They had been lepers, dirty, outcaste, shunned and lonely. But because of His word to them their lives were changed and they were now made clean and respectable. They were enabled to abandon their former outcaste ways, and lift up their heads and mix with decent society. All this had happened to all of them through the wonder-working power of Jesus, and yet, in spite of it, most of them remained all their lives standing

148

"*at a distance*" from Him, and denying any response to His call to them to enter closer into His friendship.

There are many men and women today who come to Church and yet stand always "*at a distance*" from the Christ who is worshipped and adored there, and who is ready to pour out His blessings upon His people. They constantly resist every appeal to draw near in heart and mind to Him who is the Saviour. All their confessions of sin and adoration, their prayers and praises are uttered to One who remains ever to them simply the distant and exalted Lord and Master. But they have always thwarted, and will go on thwarting every attempt on His part to lessen the gulf across which they deal with Him and to establish a closer relationship of friendship between them and Him. Even though they have been baptised in His name and come to His supper table in company with all His people, no real sign has ever appeared in their lives that they have entered into any real and living personal dealings with the Jesus Christ whom they worship and adore. They have never opened the door of the heart that He might come in and sup with them and they with Him. They are Christ's distant people. As these ten lepers "*stood at a distance and lifted up their voices and said, Jesus, Master, have mercy upon us,*" so they stand afar off and call on Him, and remain for ever afar off.

Yet their distant prayers are answered. They obtain much help and even apparent blessing through such telephonic dealings with Jesus Christ. As he shed abroad His health and goodness and cure on this distant group of ten lepers, so He often sheds abroad His love and goodness on all and sundry within His Church today, so that even those at a distance can benefit by their distant performance of ritual within the Church. They themselves will constantly claim that their Church-going "does them good." There is a power that they seem to get from it that helps them to live honest and straight lives. Their homes are different because of this family Church-going. They experience a cleansing that gives a certain sweetness and stability to life. They are grateful for this, and constantly acknowledge in a vague and distant way that this comes from God by returning regularly to the temple to sing God's praise—as the ten lepers "*showed themselves to the priests*" so they constantly show themselves in the sanctuary on the Sabbath, and offer the things due by all respectable people out of common decency.

All this they experience. All this they do. They have much to be grateful for. To them, Christianity is indeed a marvellous and supernatural force. Yet Christ Himself has never been allowed to be their friend. Always they make sure That He remains to them the distant Healer, to be looked up to and held in honour. For them, He is undoubtedly the source of an influence that is good and healthful and cleansing in the social life of any community. Yet they have never truly bent their hearts to Him in penitence and sorrow, or opened them to Him in personal devotion. Even when at the Lord's table the minister has uttered the solemn words of invitation, "Beloved in the Lord, draw near . . .," they have still kept their distance— and yet it has "done them good" to be there.

This miracle of the cleansing of the ten lepers who stood and mostly remained afar off is repeated perpetually within the Church in every generation.

The Tragedy of the Nine

The cure of nine of these lepers brought about a deep tragedy in their lives. It might have been expected that their cure would make them, from then on, godly and thankful men, giving glory to Him who had done such great things for them. But at the end of the day only one man came to Jesus in gratitude, spoke to Him face to face, and gave glory to God. And Jesus, knowing what He had done for the others as well as for the one said, *"Were not ten cleansed? Where are the nine?"* We tend to say, "What a tragedy that Jesus should have been so disappointed and grieved!" We should perhaps rather say, "What a tragedy that these nine should so damn themselves!"

Where were they—these nine? Even Jesus Christ Himself was not sure where they were. He knew that they were cleansed, but He did not know where they stood in relation to Himself or His Father. There was still in His mind a question about them—"Where are the nine?" They were to Him, indeed, still lost. They were as lost as the Pharisees whose sin also was simply that they always kept themselves at a distance from Him.

Here is tragedy indeed. They had all been blessed by Him,

but only in one case had His blessing brought a man to lasting faith, and into that real living friendship with Himself which ultimately saves men. The miraculous power of Christ worked wonders in ten lives, but only in one case was the miraculous power received and used to the glory of God, for only in one case was Jesus sure of the future destiny of this man. *"Were not ten cleansed? Where are the nine?"*

Moreover the final effect of the wonderful cure Jesus worked on the nine men was to put them further away from Him than ever before. That morning before their cure, when the leprosy was eating away at their bodies and desperation eating away at their hearts, there was some chance that their misery and desperation might yet drive them closer to the One who could cure them. But after the cure came, they needed Him now less than ever, and they obviously heeded Him the less. The very miracle accomplished on them sealed their undoing. The very gift He gave them kept them from coming to Himself the giver, and enabled them to keep between themselves and Him that distance that meant their damnation. The miracle confirmed them in their distant independence of their Lord, and made them an even greater problem to Him than they had been before. How perverse is the human heart and mind, that we can take what is meant to bring us near to God, and we can make it the very means of keeping us away from God and His Christ.

This is our human tragedy not only in the sphere of grace but also in the sphere of nature. All God's natural gifts to us, from the beauty and bounty of this created world, to the fruits of human culture and philosophy and science, are meant to bring us to Himself the giver of them all. Thus God through all the good things with which He fills our life wants to have fellowship with us. His gifts are meant to be received and enjoyed by us with a faith that constantly acknowledges the divine hand that bestows all upon us. But what happens? We accept God's gifts and forget the Giver. We enjoy God's gifts without allowing them to raise our hearts to Him in faith and gratitude. And thus it is that the more God gives us, the more absorbed we become in His gifts and the less interested in the Giver. Therefore the more we get, the more we keep apart from Him. And finally we give to His gifts the adoration and love we should give to Him alone, and thus turn them into idols that confirm us in our separation from Him.

Let us remember the solemn message of this incident: However far our religious quest may have taken us in our venture of faith and obedience, however much in moral and physical blessing it has brought us whether in healing of body or attainment of character, unless at the end of the day we find ourselves bowing at the feet of Jesus Christ in adoring gratitude for all He has done for us in His pure grace, then there is still a question mark in His mind about us. If He does not know where we are, then we are indeed lost, no matter how far we have travelled, or how much we have troubled, and how much we have taken and enjoyed of His bounty and goodness.

The Miracle of the One

Yet one leper was different from the other nine. There was one in whom the experience of being cured brought an immediate and true acknowledgement of the goodness of God, and a new desire to come near to Him by whom he had been given so much.

"*Then one of them, when he saw that he was healed, turned back, praising God with a loud voice; and he fell on his face at Jesus' feet, giving him thanks.*"

A miracle had taken place in this man's heart and soul as well as in his body. God's goodness, instead of making him independent of God now rather brings him closer to God, and to Jesus in whom he has begun to see the source of all God's goodness. This miraculous inward change that he has allowed to come upon his heart and mind, is faith. And Jesus when he saw it was thrilled at the sign of the true salvation that had been worked in this life. "*Rise and go your way*" He said, "*your faith has made you well.*" The other nine though they had to an extent been made well by Jesus did not have the faith that enables men to give God His true place in life and to see and commune with Him as He comes to give Himself to them in His Son.

This is the powerful change faith can bring about in the whole life and character of the man to whom it is given. It draws a man near to Jesus Christ in fellowship and friendship.

Nowhere is the close relationship that faith gives us with Christ more beautifully and simply expressed than in one of the prayers at the communion service. "Eternal God, our heavenly Father, who admittest thy people into such wonderful communion that, partaking by a divine mystery of the body and blood of Thy dear Son, they should dwell in Him and He in them." Faith is this inward openness of heart and life before the grace of God in Christ, that enables Jesus Christ now to give Himself to us and to dwell in us. It banishes for ever all distance between Christ and ourselves. Moreover, when we have it, it enables us to take up a right attitude to God and His gifts and His world. Faith purifies the heart (Acts xv. 9) from the perversity with which we always tend to abuse God's gifts. It enables us to come close to God through His own gifts, so that by the gratitude and thanksgiving with which the whole of life is now permeated, all life becomes sanctified (Tit. i. 15).

This faith is God's gift to those who will indeed allow themselves to be drawn near to Him in love and gratitude and surrender, instead of standing afar off in pride and independence. The only difference between the nine and the one mentioned in this story is that the nine were Jews, and this one man was a "*foreigner.*" He had less to trust in, less to cling to, less to make him proud and independent than the Jews who had so much in their religious and moral tradition to enable them to exist without Christ Himself. Perhaps because he had less than the others to live for, he was more prepared to look at Jesus Christ in all His goodness and grace, and when a man does that, the heart begins to open, the attitude begins to change, and God's grace is shown to be more powerful than all our human perversity, and in the mystery of a new relationship of fellowship and trust men begin to be made whole again.

BLIND BARTIMAEUS

As he drew near to Jericho, a blind man was sitting by the roadside begging; and hearing a multitude going by, he inquired what this meant. They told him, "Jesus of Nazareth is passing by." And he cried, "Jesus, Son of David, have mercy on me!" And those who were in front rebuked him, telling him to be silent; but he cried out all the more, "Son of David, have mercy on me?" And Jesus stopped and commanded him to be brought to him; and when he came near, he asked him, "What do you want me to do for you?" He said, "Lord, let me receive my sight." And Jesus said to him, "Receive your sight; your faith has made you well." And immediately he received his sight and followed him, glorifying God; and all the people, when they saw it, gave praise to God.

Lk. xviii. 35–43.

Jesus was on His way up to Jerusalem to die when the healing of this poor blind man took place. "And taking the twelve, He said unto them, 'Behold we are going up to Jerusalem, and everything that is written of the Son of Man by the prophets will be accomplished. For He will be delivered to the Gentiles, and will be mocked and shamefully treated and spit upon; they will scourge Him and kill Him'."

Early in Jesus's ministry He tried to avoid being publicly hailed as the Messiah, the King of Israel. He could not then show people what it meant for Him to be this Messiah. Therefore He asked many people who believed on Him not to say too much about it.

But when He started on His last journey up to Jerusalem to His cross, He knew that He was now going to be able to show men what it really meant to be the true King of Israel. They would soon see Him crowned with thorns on His strange throne, the cross, and then raised to eternal glory. Therefore on this last journey He did not mind being hailed in public as the Messiah, and twice on the way He was openly called, "Son of David." This blind man was the first to hail Him in this way, and then, later, as He was entering Jerusalem the children spread palm branches in His way, saying, "Blessed be the King who comes in the name of the Lord" (Lk. xix. 40).

On His way to this coronation, He showed what His regal power meant. He not only healed this blind man, He also cleansed the ten lepers, raised Lazarus from the dead, and brought forgiveness and new life to Zacchaeus. These were the works of the true Son of David, King of Israel, and He could accomplish them because He was the suffering humiliated King. If He could give sight and health and life and cleansing and hope and true wealth to men, it was only because He was on His way to become truly poor and hopeless, defiled, rejected, blinded and broken in fearful dereliction.

This is one of the few miracles in which we are told the name of the man Jesus cured. Mark says here that it was Bartimaeus. That his name should be mentioned in this way probably means that he later became a well-known member, or perhaps a leader, of the Christian community, and when these miracle stories became current in the Church, they said, as they told them, that this was how our Bartimaeus first met Jesus and came into the Christian fellowship.

FAITH TRIUMPHS OVER CIRCUMSTANCES

As he drew near to Jericho, a blind man was sitting by the roadside begging; and hearing a multitude going by, he inquired what this meant. They told him, 'Jesus of Nazareth is passing by.' And he cried, 'Jesus, Son of David, have mercy on me'."

The circumstances under which Bartimaeus was forced to live would have destroyed the hope and taken the heart out of most of us. His was the life of a poor blind beggar, dependent on friends to lead him daily to some miserable begging stance to pass his time howling out for charity, alongside other numerous hoarse and wretched competitors, to a world hardened in its feeling because such misery was all too common. He could not move about with any freedom. Neither could he mingle with the excited crowds that moved about the country after Jesus, nor could he have seen with his own eyes the wonderful works of God that were being accomplished. He had not even the inspiration that could come from considering the lilies of the field or the birds of the air. Yet he believed that God could and would come to him to break into the narrow confines of his small and wretched world with a mercy and power that could surprise even his own faith. Because he expected great things from God he refused to share the sordidness and bitternesss of heart and soul that others allowed such circumstances to drive them into. The story of what happened when Jesus visited Jericho and passed by Bartimaeus is the story of the miraculous upsurge of this expectant and excited faith under these most soul-destroying circumstances.

It is obvious that for some time before this Bartimaeus's faith and hope must have become centred on Jesus of Nazareth. He must have heard about Jesus as he sat by the roadside from day to day, and he must have thought a great deal about Him. This is how he came to be the first man ever to give Jesus His true title of Messiah when He drew near. He must have known something about the teaching that the Rabbis gave in the Synagogues about what the Messiah would do when He came. One passage in the Bible that appealed to him was the place that told of how the Messiah, the Son of David, would be given as a covenant to the people, a light to the nations, to open the eyes that are blind" (Is. XLII. 6–7). He felt sure that that was God's promise to himself, and he became excited when he heard of how Jesus was giving other blind people their sight. He waited for God to send the Son of David his way. He could not walk about seeking Jesus. But he could nourish this faith and hope in his heart and pray and expect that God would honour it. His expectation was intense. Whenever a likely crowd passed along the road he asked what the noise meant. Many a time he was disappointed. Sometimes he heard rumours that the crowd coming along the road might be Jesus and His disciples, but when they drew near and he asked about them, it turned out to be either some Roman soldiers, or some merchants' caravan or some Bedouin families on the move. But he kept on seeking and praying, and one day the promise that had so kindled his faith and hope was fulfilled. "What's that noise?" he asked. "Oh," they said, "it's Jesus, the carpenter fellow from Nazareth who has been teaching and supposed to be doing all these miracles." Immediately, Bartimaeus was on his feet, desperate and excited, with an outburst of exultant faith, *"Jesus, Son of David, have mercy on me."*

Many of us complain that the circumstances under which we have to live our lives today are neither conducive nor helpful to faith in God. We mourn over this soulless machine age in which the individual is made to feel he is simply one small easily replaceable part in a huge production unit which needs neither his soul nor his individuality but simply the mechanical impulse he can apply in the little place assigned to him. But blind Bartimaeus had less to encourage faith and hope in his heart than the most perplexed of us today. Yet he was full of a faith that nothing in his hard circumstances could suppress. He might have become soured and embittered, yet he was able to resist every such temptation through a sheer vitality of purpose that turned the dullness of this waiting into a glorious preparation for a certain final triumph. We too can become "more than conquerors" (Rom. VIII. 37) in this grim battle with environment if we too will allow the Word of God with its promises to possess our minds and hearts with the hope that it spontaneously creates. If we thus turn our minds and our affections always towards Jesus Christ Himself, He will create within us the same intense and expectant seeking which He Himself never disappoints, and which arises from the very knowledge that it seeks Him who has already found us and is coming to meet us.

ENCOUNTER

"Jesus of Nazareth is passing by."

Bartimaeus sought Jesus with heart and mind and soul and all the strength he had. But the encounter he had with Jesus that day by the roadside was not the result of his seeking. It took place only because Jesus "passed by." Matthew has a significant verse describing the activity of Jesus in Galilee: "And Jesus went about all the cities and villages, teaching in their synagogues and preaching the gospel of the kingdom, and healing every disease and every infirmity" (Mt. IX. 35). He did not stay in one spot and wait for people to come to Him. He did not confine Himself to the synagogues. He moved about everywhere, *"passing by"* as it were, within the reach of everybody. Every city and every village had its opportunity. Is this not what He does today? Jesus still teaches "in our synagogues." Indeed the most likely place for us to be met by Him is within our "houses of God." But He also goes about "all the cities and villages," even today *"passing by"* within the reach of many who either do not have the ability or the inclination to go near a place of worship. Few men in our own land can escape at some time being confronted by the fact that Jesus of Nazareth is there near them, within the reach of their notice, and if they will, of their faith. In all kinds of ways apart from the direct preaching of the Word in the Church, they are confronted by His name and His challenge, perhaps through their contact with Christian homes or individuals, through the agency of books, the theatre, the wireless and television, perhaps especially when they are faced with moral and political and economic choices and judgments that are going either to hurt or help their fellow men with whom Jesus has strange ways of identifying Himself. After all, even Pontius Pilate sitting at his desk at his routine business of deciding the issues that affected the human lives whose welfare he so often disregarded, was one day confronted by Jesus Himself, and before he knew where he was, he found that Jesus was the victim of his carelessness and cynicism and brutality. We do not need always to be Church-goers in order to be within the sphere where *"Jesus of Nazareth is passing by."* And sometimes, as on the first Easter Sunday evening, He can pass through doors that have been shut. He can even encounter men who have been deliberately trying to exclude Him.

There are many people within the Church who first met Him in this way outside the Church. But Jesus seeks the same living encounter with those of us who have been brought up all our days within the fellowship of the Church. Within the Church we continually hear about Jesus Christ. We talk about Him, discuss Him, and we come to conclusions and decisions about Him in theory. But unless He brings Himself into a living encounter with us personally, then in spite of all our decisions and conclusions about Him, we still remain not deeply affected by Him in the very aspects of our lives that most need transformation. Indeed a great deal of our talk within the Church about Jesus Christ, our Sunday school work, our Bible Class work, our study and discussion together is simply a preparation for the tremendous hour when this same Jesus of whom we have been talking and thinking so much, will Himself on His way through the world pass by us and confront us, and put Himself with all the new power of His Kingdom within the reach of that faith and hope that His own promises have perhaps already stirred up within us. Unless we have shared to some extent with Bartimaeus in the thrill he felt when they annouced to him at last that *"Jesus of Nazareth is passing by,"* we should indeed ask ourselves if our Christian life has really begun.

CHALLENGE

This encounter by the wayside brought to Bartimaeus a challenge in response to which he could decide his whole future and perhaps his eternal destiny. From one point of view, of course, Jesus had already decided all this by coming and putting Himself within Bartimaeus's call and reach. But from another point of view, Bartimaeus had to give and express his own decision about Jesus. He had to stop Him and lay hold of Him. That Jesus should bring Himself within Bartimaeus's reach meant for him a moment of gracious opportunity. But it was also an infinitely serious moment of choice. Any man who lives at the foot of a mountain can put off deciding whether or not to accept the challenge to climb to the top of it. If he puts off his decision till next day or till next year he knows that the mountain will still be there next day or next year with the same challenge. The mountain awaits his choice. But Christ does not await our choice like that. He is one who is *"passing by"* as He confronts us with a personal, lordly, urgent and gracious offer and call that cannot be treated like the challenge of a mere object or mere ideal.

The decision we have to make in the face of such a gracious challenge is not always easy. Bartimaeus at that moment had to refuse to be put off by serious difficulties that were, even at the last moment, put in his way. As he cried out to Jesus for mercy, *"Those who were in front rebuked him telling him to be silent."* Perhaps some in the crowd were angry at the blind vagabond for disturbing with his eager scream, the talk that was going on. Or perhaps they did not want to be involved in the political implications of calling Jesus the true King of Israel—especially when there were Roman soldiers and agents moving round. They told him to hold his tongue. Even Jesus seemed to ignore him at this stage. But he was not put off and in desperation he shouted out with even more noise and shrill eagerness.

Then and only then did Jesus stop. Perhaps He had wanted Bartimaeus to prove his faith in this way in order that He could be sure of him before He stopped. The fact that He did stop only after Bartimaeus's desperate and continued shouting should encourage us to go on repeating to Him with added urgency the prayers that He seems hitherto to have ignored.

The other accounts of this incident now show us Bartimaeus encouraged by the crowd, and so overcome with excitement that he threw off his outer coat as he came to Jesus. But if his faith has been already well tested there is an even more decisive test in the question that followed from Jesus, *"What do you want me to do for you?"* Then Bartimaeus had to confess, before His Lord and before men, his faith that Jesus was powerful and loving and great enough to meet all his need. *"Lord, let me receive my sight."*

"What do you want me to do for you?" In this question is the most searching challenge Jesus puts to any man today. How far are we prepared to open our life to Him? The whole quality of our Christian life is decided not so much by our keenness to do things for Jesus Christ as by our willingness to let Him first do things for us. As we read through the New Testament or hear the Word of God preached to us, we are constantly being given all kinds of promises in which Christ Himself assures us of His power to keep us from falling, to make us cheerful and confident in heart in spite of the worst circumstances, to make our witness tell for Him in our surroundings. In all such promises He is confronting us afresh and asking us as He did Bartimaeus *"What do you want me to do for you?"* It would be a very serious rejection of His love and power if we professed ourselves willing to take only a little when He offers us so much.

DISCIPLESHIP

"And immediately he received his sight and followed him, glorifying God; and all the people, when they saw it, gave praise unto God."

This is the outcome of our yielding to His grace. Jesus goes before us in the way He wants us to go and calls us constantly to follow Him. He is the Good Shepherd of all His people, and when the Good Shepherd leads His sheep out into the world, "He goes before them, and the sheep follow Him, for they know His voice (Jn. x. 4). This is how the Christian life is lived in this world. Through all the perplexing paths, in the midst of all the complex situations we have to face, He chooses the way. It is a way that often we are too blind and ignorant to be able to choose for ourselves. But He goes before us and calls us. If we follow Him in this way, our life is bound to glorify God, and indeed to lead others to praise God. We may not understand how it is working out in this way. In following the Good Shepherd we have often to walk by faith, believing where we cannot see, obeying where we do not understand. But if He goes before us and we hear His voice and follow Him, how can it happen otherwise than that we should share in the ultimate triumph of Jesus Christ, and find the glorious end for which we are created and redeemed?

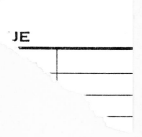